CAMBRIDGE LIBRARY COLLECTION

Books of enduring scholarly value

Cambridge

The city of Cambridge received its royal charter in 1201, having already been home to Britons, Romans and Anglo-Saxons for many centuries. Cambridge University was founded soon afterwards and celebrates its octocentenary in 2009. This series explores the history and influence of Cambridge as a centre of science, learning, and discovery, its contributions to national and global politics and culture, and its inevitable controversies and scandals.

Early Collegiate Life

First published in 1913, John Venn's collection of writings describes college life in the early days of the University of Cambridge. Venn, a leading British logician and moral scientist, was president of Gonville & Caius College, and had been a student at Cambridge in the 1850s. This volume of 'reminiscences of a reading man' contains articles he contributed to the college magazine, The Caian and speeches and addresses given at College Chapel and Hall. These are interspersed with letters written by seventeenth- and eighteenth-century Cambridge scholars, and embedded in a commentary that provides additional insights into student life and university politics. He also includes, as an appendix, 'College Life and Ways Sixty Years Ago', recounting his own student experiences. Ranging from the Elizabethan to the Victorian era, Early Collegiate Life offers an honest and delightful glimpse into the daily lives of Cambridge scholars of the past.

Cambridge University Press has long been a pioneer in the reissuing of out-of-print titles from its own backlist, producing digital reprints of books that are still sought after by scholars and students but could not be reprinted economically using traditional technology. The Cambridge Library Collection extends this activity to a wider range of books which are still of importance to researchers and professionals, either for the source material they contain, or as landmarks in the history of their academic discipline.

Drawing from the world-renowned collections in the Cambridge University Library, and guided by the advice of experts in each subject area, Cambridge University Press is using state-of-the-art scanning machines in its own Printing House to capture the content of each book selected for inclusion. The files are processed to give a consistently clear, crisp image, and the books finished to the high quality standard for which the Press is recognised around the world. The latest print-on-demand technology ensures that the books will remain available indefinitely, and that orders for single or multiple copies can quickly be supplied.

The Cambridge Library Collection will bring back to life books of enduring scholarly value (including out-of-copyright works originally issued by other publishers) across a wide range of disciplines in the humanities and social sciences and in science and technology.

Early Collegiate Life

JOHN VENN

CAMBRIDGE
UNIVERSITY PRESS

CAMBRIDGE UNIVERSITY PRESS

Cambridge, New York, Melbourne, Madrid, Cape Town, Singapore,
São Paolo, Delhi, Dubai, Tokyo

Published in the United States of America by Cambridge University Press, New York

www.cambridge.org
Information on this title: www.cambridge.org/9781108000444

© in this compilation Cambridge University Press 2009

This edition first published 1913
This digitally printed version 2009

ISBN 978-1-108-00044-4 Paperback

EARLY COLLEGIATE LIFE

LONDON AGENTS:

SIMPKIN, MARSHALL AND CO. LTD.

EARLY
COLLEGIATE LIFE

JOHN VENN, Sc.D., F.R.S., F.S.A.

President of Gonville and Caius College.

CAMBRIDGE:

W HEFFER AND SONS LTD.

1913

PREFACE.

The articles in the following volume were mostly contributed, during the last twenty years, to the College Magazine, *The Caian.* Others were delivered as addresses or speeches in the College Chapel and Hall. As was natural and suitable under the circumstances, the individual details and the personalities described or referred to, were mostly those of members of our own foundation. From this point of view I hope that these studies will serve to encourage others to enquire into the past history of whatever corporation they may belong to; and, in particular, to trace in the course of the events so displayed the main currents of the stream of national history.

But though many of the illustrations here offered may be drawn from a somewhat narrow field, the picture of early college life which I have endeavoured to portray is, I hope, a fairly general and truthful one. It should be clearly understood that the social distinctions and pretensions which to some extent prevail at present, as between one College and another, had very little significance in early days. There was no college, as I believe there was hardly any school, which was supposed to be predominantly frequented by "gentlemen's sons."

Such distinctions as existed were mainly, at bottom, topographical; that is, were dependent on the part of the country from which the students were drawn. There was also a real, though temporary, influence sometimes to be traced in the personality of a dominant Master or Tutor. A good example of this is to be found in the Romanist reaction described in the "Elizabethan Episode." On the whole the several Colleges may be considered to have been doing similar work, and doing it with similar efficiency, throughout the period in question.

CONTENTS.

I.

A COLLEGE BIOGRAPHER'S NIGHTMARE

(As described after dinner).

. . . It was a strange encounter altogether, as such experiences are apt to be; but I think there was a certain moral in it. What I had been doing or reading, to prompt such fancies, I will not undertake to say; but the scene took the form of a sort of Vision of Judgment. The locality in which I found myself was rather puzzling to me. It was not this Hall, nor was it our Chapel, though there were features in it which resembled them both; but enlarged beyond all recognition. It was filled from end to end with a vast crowd, which seemed to stretch out interminably in rank beyond rank.

The occupants evidently came from many, and some from remote districts of the country; and by their dress and deportment seemed to extend from very early times down to our own day. There were medieval prelates amongst them: some of these of saintly aspect: men—as I felt sure—, of State, and learning and piety. Others of them, however, were clad in warlike garb:—I noticed one stalwart Irish archbishop, beneath whose priestly garments, as those about made hasty way for him, I caught the glint of a coat of mail. And there was much

B

blood on the sword of a certain lordly bishop of a neighbouring diocese. There were many monks, too, in the throng; mostly Benedictines, in their black garb, from the once famous Houses of Norwich and Bury; mingled with Cluniacs from Lewes, and a group of Augustinian canons in their sober garments. Not a few of the monks had held office as abbots or priors, and I thought that one or two had mitres on their shaven heads. Others, I felt sure, must have stood high in the courts of Rome and Avignon. Here and there was a friar, grey or black. And there were not a few seminary priests, from Douay, Rheims and Valladolid, lurking in the throng; some of these, I noticed, had halters round their necks. Mixed with all these was many a gay and gallant gentleman, some with the velvet cloak, ruff and rapier which marked them as of Elizabethan date; others in the bag wig and coloured coat, of later times. Some of their faces did not seem quite strange to me: could I have seen them anywhere on these walls? But the bulk of the crowd before me was composed of Anglican clergy, mostly in cassock, wig and bands:—as to whether they would consent to wear the surplice also, there was evidently a bitter dispute. They seemed to fill the room, in crowds past all counting.

There was evidently some matter of common interest pervading that strange assembly, but what this was did not seem at first apparent. There was a universal hum of deep dissatisfaction from far and near, which gradually assumed a tone of bitter complaint and remonstrance. It was directed against some one whose name I tried in vain to catch, who, they declared, had scandalously misdescribed their careers in life. Some of them urged complaints which were perhaps not altogether without ground. But, little as one is apt to be surprised on such an occasion, it did seem to me that some of the objectors were a little touchy and unreasonable. One complained that he had held a rectory, and "that fellow had put him down as a vicar"; another had preached a sermon, "and a visitation sermon, too," and no notice taken of it. There were perpetual curates who had been described as if they were merely transitory. And so on. Nor did the laymen seem better pleased. There were squires who had been called yeomen, yeomen who had been called farmers, and so on, upwards and downwards. More than one portly country gentleman remarked that he should have thought that the dignity of the King's Commission of the Peace might at least be mentioned if the security of the country was to be upheld. Somewhere, in the midst of the throng I saw the gold-headed end of a cane violently shaken, and from beneath came a voice complaining that the holder had been F.R.C.P.; and that instead of an 'F' he was insulted with a scurvy 'M.' One pointed to a portrait on the wall, with a name attached; "They dare to call that *me*!" Some remarked that, though there was a monument to attest the fact, no notice of death was recorded.

Another, in a threatening tone, asserted that years before his death he had been foully killed by his biographer. Many of them had been studying some authority which they called 'D.N.B.'; but their complaints were not so much directed at the blunders which they said they found there, as against a certain delinquent who 'ought to have prevented such mistakes.'

Their attitude grew ever more and more menacing, and became so persistently directed against myself, as one after another pressed forwards, that I began to get alarmed. Then, with that strange intuition which one is apt to display at such moments, I suddenly reckoned up their number. I forget the exact figure, but it amounted to nearly 9000. Hardly had I done so when there came, from far and near, a simultaneous yell: "That's the man, there he is!" Then the truth flashed on my mind. They were the men whose lives I had written, and I awoke with a scream.

II.

'THE MEMORY OF OUR BENEFACTORS.'

(Address delivered on the occasion of the 550th anniversary of the foundation of the College, June 22, 1898.)

I have been deputed to propose a Toast, or rather a Memory, of the kind usually drunk in silence; for, of the many included within its scope, few indeed are within our present reach : —to be encouraged by our praise, or warmed by our thanks. It is the Memory of our Benefactors : of that great cloud of witnesses,— witnesses to the nearness of the present and the past,—which compass us about in every ancient English Institution, whether religious, civic, or academic. They are a very numerous body, and include almost every rank and station in life. Our Commemoration Service, long as it may seem, literally does not contain a tithe of those who "in their day bestowed charitably for our comfort of the temporal things given to them." The small and the great are there.

Take a few representative cases to illustrate the variety of age, condition, and motives, under which these gifts have been made. Here is a broken-hearted mother, in despair at the sudden and violent death of her only son. Dean Nowell, of St. Paul's, gives the account, and I should spoil it by repeating it in any words but his own. He says: "The mother fell into sorrows uncomfortable; whereof I, being of her acquaintance, having intelligence did with all speed ride unto her house near to Hoddesdon, to comfort her the best I could. And I found her crying or rather howling continually, Oh my son! my son! And when I could by no comfortable words stay her from that cry and tearing of her hair, God, I think, put me in mind at the last to say: 'Comfort yourself, good Mrs. Frankland, and I will tell you how you shall have twenty good sons to comfort you in these your sorrows which you take for this one son.' To the which words only she gave ear, and looking up, asked, 'How can that be?' And I said unto her, 'You are a widow, rich and now childless, and there be in both Universities so many poor toward youths that lack exhibition; for whom, if you would found certain fellowships and scholarships, to be bestowed upon studious young men, who should be called Mrs. Frankland's scholars, they would be in love toward you as dear children, and will most heartily pray to God for you during your life; and they and their successors after them, being still Mrs. Frankland's scholars,[1] will honour your memory for ever and ever." This being said, "I will," quoth she, "think thereupon earnestly." That was the origin of one of our endowments; and there is little doubt that, if

---

[1] It does not seem to have occurred to the good Dean that some future Commission would simplify matters by retaining the endowments of the various Scholarships, and suppressing the names of the donors.

we knew as much of the facts in other cases, we should find that such a story of a broken heart, or of the hope deferred that makes the heart sick, lay behind the dry legal phrases of not a few of the dusty deeds in our College treasuries. Here again is some solid citizen of Norwich or of London, who has accumulated an honest fortune; and is making up his mind, in a comfortable state of well-being and well-doing, how to dispose of some of it. He is advised that the exhibition of a young scholar,—one of the "poor toward youths" of Dean Nowell,—would be a wise and useful way of employing some of his surplus wealth. In early times a considerable part of the endowments came from men of the trading class who had no apparent connexion with any college. Here it is a wealthy bishop or archbishop who is aiming at an increase in the number of the learned clergy. Here a statesman, who wants to encourage the canonists and civilians. Here a poor priest, in same far off parsonage, whose thoughts fondly revert to the library of his youth; and who, in giving us a book or two, gives perhaps all he has to leave. Not a few of the ancient MSS. still on our shelves belong to this class. Here it is a knight or a country squire, who conveys land or an advowson, or founds a chantry under the patronage of the college. Bishop Shaxton, of Salisbury, coming back here to die in his old age, leaves the rent of a house "to solace the company at home yearly at Christmas." A young student, cut off in his commencing career, leaves a cup, that his memory may not die out amongst his comrades. One gives with the cheerful recollection of well-spent hours : he thinks it " his duty to cast in his mite into that fund which he has so abundantly enjoyed." Another, in a spirit of remorseful retrospect, recalls " the twenty unprofitable years I spent there by my negligence and folly."

I suppose that any one who listens to such a long Roll-call, stretching over century after century, as that which constitutes a list of College Benefactors, inevitably falls into an attitude of criticism. He begins to judge the wisdom of the ends designed : the foresight of the means provided. Has it ever occurred to you, Gentlemen, to conceive this attitude of judgment reversed ? If that varied host of charitable donors could be raised to life again, —purged, we may assume, of prejudice and narrowness, but retaining each the special interest which he once had at heart,—and constituted a commission to enquire into the way in which we had used their benefactions, how should we fare at their hands? I appre- hend that such an assembly is one which few of us here present could face without a certain anxiety. Not a man in this room but has bene- fitted in some way, at school or at college, by the fruits of endowment; and some amongst us have fed freely on them. But those of us who are in the position of trustees might well feel some trepidation. Personally, I think that something might turn on the question as to who should preside over such a commission. If it were Bateman, bishop of Norwich, we might entertain some hope; for he was a thorough man of the world, versed in the ways of royal and of papal courts : he would know well how to make allowance for weakness, and for changes of thought and feeling. But with Dr. Caius in the chair it would be another matter. He was a severe man : rigid in his own conception of duty ; stern in his exaction of duty from others. He had too a deep love and veneration for the past.

On one point indeed, and that an important point, we should not have much to fear. The stewardship has on the whole always been sound and conscientious. Each succeeding age has rightly regarded itself as a trustee : bound to guard carefully what it had received from those before, and to hand it on undiminished to those who came after. No estate, I believe, even in the worst of times, has been lost by fraud or negligence. There has been little or none of that greed which sacrifices the future to the present, and which was sometimes such a scandal in the monasteries and in many civic corporations.

But in matters of sentiment and association rather than of property, it would be far otherwise, and the story of neglect and loss is a sad one. As I walk by our chapel door I seem to see William Rougham, second master of the college, who beckons me in with an air of authority, and introduces me to a small but dignified assemblage. Rougham himself is a man of mark ; wealthy and liberal. By his side is Henry de Spencer, the famous bishop of

Norwich, the great warrior prelate of his age, fresh from his rout and slaughter of the Norfolk rebels. There too is John of Ufford, son of the Earl of Suffolk, the first known fellow-commoner of the college. They are examining, with a certain curiosity, our present display of glass;—but they want to know what has become of the windows which each of them presented 500 years ago. Rougham has some cause to feel aggrieved, for the window which he placed there expressly recorded that he was the builder of the chapel; and as to the bishop, it is perhaps as well for us that he is not now stalking about here in his coat of mail.

I slink away, and seek refuge in the library. There, again, is a distinguished company. William Lindwood, bishop of St. Davids, who died in 1446; with his contemporaries, the archdeacon of Norfolk and the chancellor of Salisbury; also Thomas Boleyn, master of the college, and grand uncle of the unfortunate queen. There also are two or three of our earliest fellows ; rectors of important parishes in London and elsewhere. They frankly admit that the ancient library they knew so well, and amongst whose chained volumes they used to work, had to go. But could no place be found for the windows which each of them placed in the ancient room ? The bishop hints that he should have thought that the author of the Provincial Constitutions was one of whose connection with them any college might have been glad to retain such evidence. I evade the subject by begging the bishop to inspect our valuable collection of MSS., assuring him that he will still find on our shelves nearly every book he remembers to have read here; and, offering to fetch the librarian, I escape by the ancient staircase. As I descend I am stopped by the awful presence of Dr. Caius himself, who sternly reminds me that,—as he has recorded in the *Annals*,—on that staircase used to be a window of historic interest. It contained the likenesses of two of the De La Poles, formerly fellow-commoners here, members of that great ducal house of Suffolk which was exterminated under Henry VIII. I try this Hall; and it is the same tale. There is John Crouch, dean of Chichester; one of the earliest donors to the University Library; in fact one of its founders. With him are others of our earliest fellows. Again, it is a question of the windows. The dean remarks, with stately courtesy, that they are doubtless the very best we can now produce: but where, they would like to know, are the windows which they placed in the ancient building?

It is a sad story. We have records of some 18 or 20 windows: each with some personal memory clinging to it: each recording the student life here of some departed scholar, or of some ancient worthy of Church or State; and, so far as we know, not one square inch of any one of them is now in existence.[1]

---

[1] There is reason to believe that three small glass coats of arms, long hidden away in a bedroom in the master's lodge, but now placed in a better position in a window on the ground floor, are the remains of those given by Dr. Dorington.

I slip into the chapel again, after making sure that the stalwart bishop is gone. There I find Anthony Disberow, former fellow, enquiring about the brass eagle which he gave as a lectern. 'You might think it a poor thing,' he says, 'compared with what you now turn out at Birmingham: but it was mine own; and there was a bit of sentiment about it, which is perhaps the reason why you would not let it remain. It bore an inscription testifying to the "eternal love" which I felt towards my old college.' Near him is another former fellow, Francis Dorington, of Dr. Caius' time: an unruly member of the house in his day. 'I know,' he says sadly, 'that I got and gave many a hard blow in my time, before you could get rid of me; and the record of my doings survives in the archives of the State Paper Office: but could you not also have preserved the record of my reconciliation? In after years I put a glass window in this chapel, to replace an earlier one already destroyed. It bore the arms of Gonville, of Bateman, and of Caius, as well as my own arms; and the simple inscription "amice fecit"; to intimate that old animosities had died out, and that I hoped henceforth to be remembered only as a faithful son of the ancient house.'

It is a sad story; but I do not think that it is one for which the present generation has cause to feel shame. That callous indifference to any sentimental or historical association may fairly be considered a thing of the past. Of late years nothing has been let pass away which could by possibility be retained; and I

know the keen interest felt in what survives.
and the jealous care with which it is preserved,
It is mainly the past which is guilty of
destroying its own past. It is not only,
or indeed mainly, those convenient scape-
goats of the disappointed antiquary, — the
Reformation and the Commonwealth,—which
are to blame. The chief destructive agencies
are of another and a humbler kind. To
characterize their constant and insidious action
we must fall back upon the old Scriptural
metaphor of the canker worm and the cater-
pillar. I do not know what are the original
Hebrew terms which have been thus translated,
but we may take it for granted that the actual
agencies the prophet had in view were the same
as those which we now call 'architect' and
'bursar.'

But such a Commission as I have supposed
might raise a more serious question than the
destruction or preservation of property. When
anyone has followed, as I have been lately doing,
the continuous but varying development, for
century after century, of an ancient institution
like ours: enquiring whence the students come
who one after another are gathered within our
walls, and whither they go as they disperse
about the world upon their various careers, he
almost inevitably has the reflection forced upon
him, at what period have the real ends of all
these endowments been best secured? The
stewardship has been good : but when have the
funds, thus carefully preserved, been admin-
istered as an enlightened founder might be

supposed to think best? In other words, when, in the long life of a college or a university, has it most nearly fulfilled the ideal of faithfully reflecting the best culture and learning of the country, and been most influential in refining that culture and extending that learning? And when has it been most successful in attracting to itself all the material in the country, in whatever station or place it could be found, that would best respond to its influences? I am no optimist, and I dare not suggest that in such a comparison the colleges or universities of this day would head the list. On the contrary, I think there are two, or perhaps three, periods in the past in which we should find ourselves excelled. I think we stand well, but we dare not claim the highest place. I can only hope that when the final judgment of History,—if any final judgment there be,—is passed upon us, it may be said that however erroneous our theories we endeavoured honestly to act upon them: that however limited and shallow our knowledge, we strove to broaden and deepen it: that in respect of the past we tried humbly to learn what it had to teach: and that in respect of the future we did what we could not to hamper it by our prejudice, confusion and error. Fifty years hence there will be occasion for a rehearsal of that judgment; and some of you younger men,—unless you go out of your way to defy the Theory of Statistics,—will have the chance to be present at it. I hope you will be lenient to us.

One guess or fancy, and I have done. What, of all the personal possessions and destructible things which the college owns now, will be in existence 500 years hence? It is doubtless an idle guess, but excusable on such an evening as this, when our unit of time is the half-century. Past experience tells us nothing here. What have we now that belonged to us 500 years ago? There is the brick-work of the chapel and of one side of the Gonville court, covered over by the modern facing of stone and out of sight; there are several MSS.; perhaps one or two pieces of plate; and a curious old astrolabe, not improbably handled by Gonville himself. That, as far as we know, is all. I like to indulge my fancy as to one or two of the things in our present possession. Five hundred years is a very long time indeed in the life-history of a college building: it is an eternity in that of most of the business which occupies us here: but it is not, or need not be, such a very long time in the existence of some material things— shall we say of a *bell*? I like to think that our successors of that far-off date may perhaps be summoned together by the same sound as we have heard; and that this, our latest gift, may still be flinging forth its solemn notes of an evening:—it may be through the smoke of square miles of crowded city: it may be through the gathering mists of a region which has reverted to its ancient condition, and has again become a waste of swamp and fen.

And there is another fancy which I like to indulge. There is a familiar adage about the laws and the songs of a country, and their respective importance. May we give a rough rendering of this into Academic phraseology by saying that any man, even a young man, may draft a college statute, and that any man, even an old man, may live to see that statute repealed? But he who puts together the winged words of some song which catches on, and he who strengthens the pinions of its flight by fitting it to some subtle combination of sweet sounds, are workmen of another stamp. I like to fancy that our far off successors will listen to the familiar chorus of our *Carmen*,—set perhaps to some new and strange accessories of musical accompaniment, —that they will toast the memory of the composers, and that perhaps the college annalist and historian of that day will be called on to tell the company who the men were who gave them that lasting benefaction. Gentlemen: I give you the Memory of our past Benefactors.

III.

MOTIVES AND IDEALS OF THE EARLY FOUNDER.

(Address delivered in the College Chapel, after the Commemoration Service, Dec. 21, 1894.)

I have now and then indulged the fancy, whether, — if some Supreme Power were to grant us for once the privilege of taking our holiday ramble, not to the *place* but to the *time* of our choice,—of spending a few weeks in this or that century according to our choice,—we should elect to go forwards or backwards. If we may indulge in such a freak of fancy, the preference would perhaps largely turn upon the question of temperament, and therefore to some extent upon that of age. Many a buoyant and youthful spirit would gladly rush to the front, with the conviction that it not merely contains the key to all truth, but that it represents the outcome of all past experience. Perhaps if one were addressing such an assembly as commonly fills this chapel, sympathy would prompt one to side with such a sentiment. But to most of us elder men, I apprehend, the centre of interest has shifted, or is shifting, from the van to the rear.

This is an idle fancy, but it may serve as an introduction to the only treatment of academic endowments appropriate here and now. Shall

c

we then, for the few minutes available, endeavour not to lay down what such endowments
should be, or perhaps eventually will be, but
simply to ascertain something as to the motives,
intentions and lives of those who actually established them? We will try to lift a corner of the
veil which seems to shroud the far past, and to
strain our eyes through the mists of four centuries, in order to make out,—as to such men as
those whose names have just been sounding in
our ears,—what lives they lived within our
walls, and what motives prompted them to
their benevolence. Something can be done in
this way; though those words, which seem to
me to breathe a fresh pathos every time I hear
them, are still true of many :—"There be, which
have no memorial; who are perished as though
they had never been."

Shall we, for one thing, try to picture to
ourselves what the life here was, 400 years ago?
Further back than that we cannot go with
much confidence. In the existent state of our
records, and of most other sources of personal
information, the outlines then begin to crumble
away. In place of the words and deeds of living
men, we are left in possession of nothing
beyond a few names and dates. But so far
back, our footing is to some extent sure. We
may picture to ourselves a small assemblage of
probably 20 or 25 persons, constantly meeting
within these very walls, not only for religious,
but for all corporate purposes. We know not
merely their names, but something of their
surroundings, whence they came and from what

position in society, and still more, what career
they followed, and what part they played in life.
The corporate feeling was of course very strong:
far stronger than with us, who have so many
links of connection with the outside world. We
must not forget that they too had a past behind
them, to which they strove to bind themselves
with many an obit mass and prayer. And their
dead lay closer to them than is the case with us.
Some were laid to their rest here: others in the
aisle of St. Michael's hard by. Those of their
comrades who died in college, whom they com-
memorated, and on whose souls they prayed
that God might have mercy, were lying close at
hand.

In such a commemoration service as we
publicly hold here we cannot record any but
the prominent names, "the famous men." But
the aggregate made up by the host of the
unrecorded is very great, and it is of them that
I would rather speak now. Gifts of small actual
value were almost universal. It is noticeable
how rare it is to find an ancient Will of one of
the members of our older societies here, in
which the thoughts of the testator do not
revert, at the last, with fond and grateful
remembrance to the house or hall in which the
seed-time of his early days had been spent.
The parish priest, as so many of these men
were, had but little to give. But after he has
made mention of the altar or rood-light of the
church where he had been baptized, and the
tower or the chancel of that wherein he had
ministered, or celebrated his first mass, his

thoughts generally wandered back to his student's days, and he pondered how he could help those who were struggling along the same path of poverty and trial which he had once trodden himself. That is the history of not a few of our MSS. Shall we be far wrong if we picture to ourselves some poor priest, passing away in a distant parsonage, his mind perhaps already disturbed by the commencing shocks of the great religious earthquake and prematurely aged by the scenes of war and famine and pestilence through which he had passed? He recalls the hours he had spent as a youth in the chilly garret which served for a library, as he made the most of the brief daylight, and he remembers how he had longed in vain for a sight of this or that volume which the frugality of many later years has since enabled him to procure. So he adds it to the store on our shelves, and shows his sense of the real value of his gift by the precautions he asks for its safe custody. Many of our books are suggestive of details in the life and death of the far past. Now and then there is some record of the gift in the *Annals* of the College, or in the lists recorded in our library; but more often we can only infer the fact from the name on a blank page or from the last will of the donor. This is not mere guesswork. Take an instance or two from the records in the Probate Courts. Thus Geoffrey Champney, once a Fellow,—who died in 1472,—after making bequests to the Church of Cromer, where he had been vicar, and to that of St. Stephen, Norwich, which he served till then, and leaving small legacies to the prior and to each monk of the Charter House and of Sion, his dying thoughts revert to this chapel where he had so often worshipped and to the library which he knew so well. He leaves 40s. for the repair of the former, and his copy of Philip Rippington's *Homilies* to the latter, with directions that it should be chained up in its place. That book is there now, on our shelves. Perhaps it was his memory of such a gift that prompted Robert Carlton, himself a Fellow of the College, who died in Norwich 30 years afterwards, to direct that he should be buried by the side of Champney. Those who turn over our old MSS. will find in them from time to time these trifling intimations, these touches which help the annalist and biographer to transform mere names into human beings. Thus Henry Osburne, Fellow of the College in 1392, gave us a copy of *Polychronicon* of Ralph Higden. He was probably giving us of his best. On the fly-leaf is an entry, dated 1400—presumably by the proctor of the time—that this volume was the *cautio* or pledge of Henry Osburne. These pledges were very common then and long afterwards, sometimes to raise money for fees or other necessary purposes, more often as security for performing the exercises requisite for the higher degrees. Now and then the pledge consists of money or plate, but often the poor scholar's only available treasure is one of his valued books. Osburne must have left us that book; and though he himself is numbered amongst those who are as if "they had never been" as regards any public recognition, yet as one handles his book after just five centuries, one seems to be brought closer to him. Volumes have come to us in this way from many parts of the country. Some were given by the Vicar of Leeds, Henry Thomson, in 1430; others by the Rector of St. Andrew's, Holborn, in 1502; and so on. Amongst these ought in justice to be mentioned John Crucher, Fellow in 1407. The glass windows which he helped to give— presumably for this chapel—have long since been shattered and have given place to others, which in their turn have disappeared. But there is still a MS. of his gift in the University Library which Mr. Bradshaw pronounced to be the gem of the English collection.

As one thus looks backward across the chasm of four centuries one cannot help wondering sometimes whether, with these men, the wings of fancy made a similar flight forwards; and if they dared to frame any conscious hope that after such a lapse of time their own lineal successors should be meeting within the same walls, and striving somehow to get at their personal history. Probably not; for those were no times of optimism. I suspect that to most men of that day, of the convictions and temperament of the pious donor, however unshaken their own personal faith might be, despair rather than hope would seem the fitting attitude towards the future of the world. But one would fain believe that it might have been so, and that their minds could have been cheered by the conviction, somehow granted to them, that the tiny barque which they were launching on the waters would be still afloat after three such tempests as the Reformation, the Revolution, and what, to certain kinds of benefaction was almost equally fatal, the coarser Utilitarianism of recent times.

As regards the more permanent endowments — in distinction from the single gifts—the question is often asked, What exactly were the intentions of the donors? Whom did they propose to benefit, and with what ultimate object? On this point there cannot be much doubt for those who have studied the deeds of foundation. What they looked to was the encouragement of what may be called the higher professional study:—not the production, so to say, of the mere artificer, on the one hand, nor on the other, the maintenance of what is known as original research. The sheer love of speculation, of study for study's sake, must always and everywhere be the vocation of the very few, and can hardly be legislated for. The monastery, if any place, would have been the appropriate soil in which such a plant might from time to time spring up. But the founders of most of our endowments never dreamt of adding to the monastic establishments, nor contemplated any permanent residence in our buildings here. Their provisions taken together, seem to point to the design of securing that thoroughness of study which can only come of leisure, and that dignity of tone which is hardly attainable where the struggle for bread begins too soon. The object of the foundation was to stimulate that spirit, and secure those results, and then to encourage the student to go out and take his place in the struggle of the world. This points to a very different aim from that of the monastery, which kept its hold on the recruit for life.

Did then the results answer to the founders' expectations? Did the system, whilst it was in its first freshness, breed the sort of men whom they had in mind when they made their provisions? This is a question of historical facts and can only be answered by an appeal to such facts. Let us confirm ourselves to a dozen years towards the beginning of the 16th century, close upon 400 years ago. During this periods 64 men seem to have dwelt within our walls. Of one quarter of these nothing more is known: of the remaining 48 we are able to ascertain something definite. This in itself is a striking fact; for, as everyone who has edited a School or College Admission Register well knows, it is no light task to ascertain the career of three-fourths of the men who entered it as lately as a generation ago.

Of these men three became Bishops— Shaxton of Salisbury, Skipp of Hereford, and Repps of Norwich. Two others were amongst the foremost physicians of their time—Sir Wm. Butts, physician to Henry VIII., described by a contemporary as "the refuge of all students, and the chief guardian and ornament of the

University"; and Sir Thos. Wendy, physician to four successive monarchs, whose name is still in your ears. As rising to State distinction must be added Sir Nicholas Hare, Master of the Rolls and a distinguished antiquary, and Lord Morley. Sixteen were monks, of whom six probably became priors of their respective houses, and one sub-prior; one or two, on their return, were appointed teachers in their own houses, to hand on to others the instruction they had themselves received. Of course at the dispersal these men had to look elsewhere, but they mostly did not — like so many of their brethren—disappear as mere pensioners; one became Bishop of Norwich, another Dean of Ely, another prebendary of Lincoln, another a Rector in London. Of the secular clergy ten held the office of University preacher, viz. were of the limited number licensed by the University to that function, and they mostly held posts of a certain importance. One was Canon of Lincoln, two held churches in London, one in Norfolk, and so on. Add to these the Chancellor of Beverley, two canons of St. Paul's, and a man selected as one of the first Fellows on the new foundation of Cardinal College at Oxford. Eight men became parish priests; two of them in churches in the City of London, the others in Norfolk and elsewhere. Two only, as far as can be traced, belonged to the class which subsequently became relatively so numerous, viz. that of the leisured class, the country gentry, and these appear to have wished to make some return for the privilege of sojourn here. One was Nicholas Buckenham, who added to our buildings. The other, Walter Stubbe, is not certainly known as a donor, but as his brass in the ante-chapel is one of the only two ancient monuments here, it seems highly likely that he was so.

What should we say to such a roll-call of honourable and dignified success in life, had these 64 been the entry of some one recent year? The comparison is of course an unfair one. The doors of a college are thrown wider open now, and many come whose only aim is to secure the minimum qualification which will admit to a profession, or to fill up an interval of life which it is not, at the moment, seen how else to dispose of. You will understand that I am not presuming to judge whether this is, or was, what ought to be. We merely want to get at facts here. Those early benefactors, whose names have been familiar to most of us for so many years, in this building, what did they really contemplate when they gave us of their good things? and did the results, for a time at any rate, justify them in their forecast? I do not think there can be much doubt in respect of the answer to either question.

But such success in life, even when it assumes the dignified and honourable form of office and station rather than of reward, is only one element in determining the judgment. What test can we adopt of any such higher results? In such a narrow field we cannot look for brilliant originality. The men who largely add to knowledge, or improve our methods of speculation, must always be so few that their appearance will seem casual. No system can fairly have its success tested by the production of such men as these. Perhaps the best test for such a purpose is to be found in the men of the second rank, amongst the larger number who can sympathise and carry out, rather than invent, and who are prepared to take their venture on what others have set before them rather than strike out a new line for themselves.

Now the men of whom we have been speaking lived in just one of the epochs when such a test becomes appropriate. Most of them must have been called upon to part to one side or the other in the great division of the Reformation. How did they meet the crisis? Did a fair proportion of them promptly take a side, follow the dictates of conviction or conscience, and face the issue? I think, when we turn to the facts, the answer will be found to be an emphatic affirmative. We would fain head our list with a martyr, but that is denied us. We have no Latimer or Ridley or Bilney to show. But in the next rank, to speak of those who risked and who suffered short of death, there is no small number; quite enough to justify the well-known saying of Bishop Nix as to the character then borne by Gonville Hall. Confining ourselves to a period but little longer than that we considered before, I find no less than eight or nine who must be ranked in this honourable class. The number seems to me to be large, when we remember how many of the total of residents were monks, whose lifelong training made any willing change of this sort almost impossible.

As the men I have in view are mostly not of the eminence which entitles them to notice in general History, some of them indeed might be almost said to be unknown, I mention their names. The best known is Shaxton, Bishop of Salisbury, and for some time Fellow. He was prominent in the early days of the Reformation: was repeatedly imprisoned, and condemned to the stake, but escaped by recantation. John Skipp, Bishop of Hereford, went some way in the same direction, and was charged with sedition. Edward Crome was for many years Fellow, and had the high approval of Cranmer: " when he was but president of Physic Hostel his house was better ordered than all the houses in Cambridge besides." He was repeatedly in trouble for his opinions, and was imprisoned in 1554. Sir Wm. Butts, though a friend of Cranmer and decided reformer, did not, I believe, suffer. Sygar Nicholson, University printer, and for some years a resident pensioner here, suffered the most. He was long imprisoned, and is said to have been tortured with much barbarity. Dr. Warner, Fellow for some 10 years, and afterwards Rector of Winterton, went at his risk to comfort Bilney, the Norwich martyr, before his death. Simon Smith, also a Fellow, was a friend and associate here of Latimer and others of like stamp, and a prisoner for his opinions. Patmore, Smith's

rector at Hadham, Herts., was a prisoner for
two years in the Lollard's Tower, Lambeth. All
of these were more or less prominent men here,
as members of the little cluster of early Cambridge reformers—Latimer mentions several
of them when addressing his persecutors, "Do
you not hold Nicholson, Smith, Patmore, with
many others, in prison at this very hour?"
These names lie but just beneath the surface
of current history: if we were to dig lower
we should doubtless come upon others. What
a significant hint is there in the will of Thomas
Ocley, a Fellow who was cut off young in 1537.
He gives all his goods to Nicholas Ridley and
others, "to dispose of as they do know, and
shall by searching of Scripture, all affection
put away," decide. No wonder that Bishop
Nicks of Norwich gave utterance to the
ominous and often quoted description: "There
is a college in Cambridge called Gunwell Haule.
I hear no clerk that hath comen out lately of
that college but saverith of the frying panne,
tho he spake never so holely."

Time fails, or one would like to emphasize
how here, as in all such crises, we find the men
trained in any institution worthy of the name
of Liberal and Catholic, parting asunder, and
then meeting later on in hostile array. It was
so during the Romish reaction in the days of
Elizabeth, and still more so, both in religion
and politics, in the time of the Revolution.
Surely this is the stamp of the highest training.
It is not merely the dramatic interest which is
aroused by finding those who had sat side by

side here meeting again as judge and prisoner,
or facing each other in the angry struggle of
controversy or across the field of battle. Of the
hosts who gathered in support of opposing
principles at the time of the Revolution, one
could hardly say, without actual enumeration,
on which side those from our walls were found
in greatest numbers.

For a time of course those who have been
brought up under the same influences will
preponderate on one side. But if such tendency
became overwhelming and remained persistent,
then we should say that a college had sunk
to a seminary, and that doctrines had been
set above principles. We must not say that
this diversity of conviction and career was
the conscious aim of those whom we com-
memorate to-day. But I feel little doubt that
it was involved in the principles underlying
their provisions, and no doubt that it was on
the whole the outcome of their sacrifice. May
others, in the days to come, say as much of us
and of our efforts!

IV.

THE COLLEGE BENEFACTOR.

(Address delivered in the College Chapel,
Sunday, October 30, 1904.)

You have just listened to a long catalogue
of names, almost all unfamiliar to you, and
many dating from times so remote as apparently to preclude all possibility of present
reference to ourselves. Nothing as a rule
sounds more uninteresting than a roll-call of
bare names. Think with what indifference
anyone—especially a young man—glances
through the list of deaths in a newspaper!
And yet even there, if we could lift the veil
in each successive case, what a tragedy of
passion and emotion would be disclosed. Here
a career cut short at the moment when the
prize of life seemed almost within grasp; there
the catastrophe of a ruined and blasted life
recklessly cast away; here the desolation of a
loving home; there the bitterness of remorse
for conduct which nothing can now reverse.
It is well perhaps for the purposes of practical
life that no such vision in all its details is ever
granted to us.

What I want to do at present is to spend
a few minutes in trying to lift, here and there,
the thick veil which hangs between our eyes
and the lives and motives of those whose names
you have listened to in the roll-call of this

morning. It is but little we can effect in this
way. Many of the donors are known to us
almost entirely by the mere fact of their gifts.
And if we refer to the original records it is but
slight help we find. You go down into our
Treasury, and see the drawers and shelves filled
with ancient deeds, stained with the dust of
centuries. When you read them you will find
them couched in legal verbiage which really
sounds almost as though it were contrived for
the purpose of making the gift look like a sordid
bargain. Some dead man has left land or
money for the use of students, and in return
the priest, under penalties, shall sing masses
for his soul. So the words may run; but the
facts are generally far other than this whenever
we can actually succeed in getting at them.

We must here bear in mind one important
distinction between ancient and modern life.
Personal property is abundant almost everywhere now. A modern donor may sometimes
hardly know that he has drawn a large cheque,
or he who receives it know that he has done so,
except by consulting their pass-books. The
personal effects now inventoried in a single
room of any well-to-do person may far out-
number in range and value the aggregate of
what any but the really rich once had to leave
behind them.

But in old days it was far otherwise.
Some almost insignificant gift, therefore, the
mere mention of which would now raise a
smile, was a serious consideration on both
sides. It implied a real sacrifice. It demanded

anxious consideration on the part of the
giver, whether he could spare it, and consequently, called for gratitude on the part of
the receiver. He who gave a book during his
lifetime may have appreciably curtailed his own
facilities for study. He who gave an ornament
—plate for the table, a service-book for the
chapel—may have left his own home or room
perceptibly the poorer. To part with anything
would probably involve actually missing it.

A trivial instance will explain what I mean.
We of the present day hardly know what it
is really to suffer from cold, unless perhaps
briefly on a journey or some such casual
occasion. But this must have been the
medieval student's normal experience during
winter. Think what it must have been to sit
and study in an unwarmed room: to spend hours
in a library where you had with numbed fingers
to handle the heavy chained volumes: to feed
in a hall without a fire; the floor of stone and
no hangings on the wall. But this condition of
college life prevailed for centuries. Then two
benevolent men in the time of Elizabeth—
Shaxton once Bishop of Salisbury, a former
student and fellow, and Dr. Bisbey, an old
fellow-commoner—combined to relieve the dis-
comfort. A large brasier was provided, and
land was bought, the rent of which should
supply fuel. The date of the first occasion on
which the fire was lighted in the Hall is
recorded in the *Annals*, as an important event
in the College history.

Such an incident as this excites a smile

nowadays, and we might be inclined to class it with the rather perfunctory efforts of a village coal or blanket club. But the men of that day knew better. No wonder the names of the donors were gratefully recorded, and a special grace was said and a hymn of thanks sung at every meal to record the gift, and to praise the Lord "who made His ministers a flame of fire."

It is this personal element which is so interesting and so characteristic of early times. Each benefactor felt a keen sympathy with those whom he proposed to benefit; each of the latter in turn knew exactly who it was whom he had to thank. In very many cases the gift was probably the outcome of a keen recollection of discomforts and privations experienced in their own youth. Nowadays much of our charity, as of our social efforts in general, is carried on almost impersonally, through some agency or other. We may be casually asked by a stranger to contribute to some cause which we do not understand, which assists we hardly know whom, we hardly know where.[1] And the

---

[1] Take, for example, the case of our scholarships down to the time of the first University Reform Commission. The scholar at any rate knew whom he had to thank for the help he received. Doubtless the conviction that this was a *charity*, rather than a reward which he had rightly earned by his merits, had nearly faded away. And of course the obligation to pray for the soul of the founder had long been legally abrogated. The name of the donor, however, was carefully retained, and therefore the historic basis for gratitude was left intact. Contrast with this the position of the modern County Council School scholar when he comes to the University. No notion of gratitude to be displayed probably ever enters his mind. Why should it, considering the drift of much modern legislation? He considers that he has a right to what he has earned, as being first on the list. As to

recipient may have even less of personal knowledge, and consequently of rational gratitude in this relation, than the donor.

Of course there are plenty of exceptions to such a statement as the above. Do not forget that we, as a college, have abundant reason to recognise the value and the wisdom of what the *living hand* can do in the way of providing for the educational wants of the day and for the amenities of life. But, speaking generally, there can be little doubt, I think, that such a broad contrast as that sketched above is to be observed between the positions of the ancient and the modern members of such foundations. The recognition of this will help to explain much that may seem quaint, trivial and out of date in such a Commemoration service as you have listened to to-day.

Try to picture to yourself what was part of the daily life of a student, say some four or five centuries ago. Poor he was of course : the whole foundation was miserably poor compared with an average monastery. But on every side, whatever elements there were to relieve his discomforts, to brighten his daily life, and to aid him in his studies, could be assigned to some known benefactor. He came to pray in this chapel—already old in his day, for it has stood substantially the same building now for more than five centuries. Such few ornaments

praying for a soul, if such a fantastic medieval idea were suggested, it would certainly puzzle any of us to decide whose soul it ought to be :—Should we be wrong in suggesting that of the late Lord Ritchie, as the originator of County Councils, or that of some representative ratepayer?

as then existed here were all of known origin.
The glass windows, which protected from the
weather, recorded the names, the arms, and the
pious wishes of great men in the past. They
were the gift of the living to the living. Costly
vestments for the altar were the gift of Bishop
Bateman, founder of Trinity Hall, and dated
from the first building of the college. The
earlier altar vessels came from Bateman and
Somersham, the third Master; those of a somewhat later date, and still in use, were a present
from Archbishop Parker, a sign of his intimate
friendship with Dr. Caius. The brass eagle—
long since disappeared, like too many other
relics of the past—bore an inscription of the
" eternal friendship " of a former Fellow to the
foundation on which he had been reared. A
window expressly recorded the regret felt by
one of the most turbulent opponents of Dr.
Caius, and his reconciliation with his old
antagonists : and so on.

You might follow the ancient student
through the rest of the college, and observe
how, at every step of his course, and every
stage of his career, he was reminded of those
who in the past had striven to help him.

Many of the gifts came from country clergy.
A priest in the far north, who must have lived
during the Civil Wars more than 400 years ago,
left all his books to the library : doubtless his
mind reverted at the end to the quiet hours
he had once spent there. One from Hampshire
gave a sum of money to be freely lent to
students in necessity : the scholar's path was no

flowery one then. A Bishop of St. David's gave
a window to the library: as a deep student of
the old canon law he well knew its contents.
From such remote places, on every side, gifts
came dropping in.

There is a somewhat prevalent notion, I
believe, that gifts in pre-Reformation times are
to be looked on with suspicion. They are often
regarded as if they had been extorted from the
dying by the pressure of religious terrors.
There may have been something of this influence
in the case of the monasteries, especially in rude
and turbulent times. But I can find no appeal
to any such motives in the case of our colleges.
As already remarked, these were humble institutions, and did not for the most part arise until
the commencement of the reaction against the
monks and friars. In fact, they are often the
expression or the consequence of that reaction.
The tyrannous baron, whose lands are extorted
from him as a selfish precaution on his death-
bed, is, I conceive, entirely unknown in the
history of our various endowments in Cambridge.
Our "nursing fathers and nursing mothers"
were, in not a few instances, living men and
women; and, where the donors had literally
nothing to spare during life, they are generally
men who had spent their early days under all
the hardships of a student's life, and still
retained vivid recollections of the privations
from which they strove to save their successors.
Some of them, as in our own case with Edmund
Gonville, were simply parish priests, into whose
hands accident had thrown the disposal of

property. Some were flourishing merchants of
Norwich or some other great town, whose sons
or nephews were students, and who therefore
knew well what was wanted. Our buildings
were largely due to such men. Some belonged
to the well-known medieval class of statesmen
Bishops, men immersed in political affairs at
home and abroad. William Bateman, of Norwich,
who carried out and added to Gonville's bequest;
the lordly De Spencer already mentioned;
Colton, the famous Archbishop; Lynwood of
St. David's, the greatest canonist, belonged to
this class. Such men were deeply devoted to
the encouragement of sound learning and
religious education, and to securing this by
training up young men for the service of the
Church and the State.

Men and women of mark and of wealth have
thus freely contributed throughout the whole
history of our college. But, after all, these
represent relatively a very small minority of the
total. The vast majority of those whose names
would be included in a complete roll-call of
benefactors are persons like ourselves; swayed
by just the same motives as those which still
have force over every true and loyal son of his
school or college. They wished to live on in the
memory of their old comrades; to save their
successors from some of the toils and privations
which they had themselves undergone; to signify
their gratitude to those who in earlier days had
helped their own career.

Well, their ideals are not always ours; their
methods are in large part superseded; many of

the gifts which they secured for us, with painful toil and conscious self-sacrifice are nowadays heaped about us, almost encumbering us with their mass. But the spirit of the donors may remain unchanged.

It is a strange feeling, that of belonging to an ancient foundation, one which has been doing its appointed work for century after century in the past, and will, we would fain believe, continue to do so into the far and unknown future. Its whole course, as we have seen, has been, so to say, punctuated by incessant displays of the kindly sympathy of those who had once belonged to it. Scarcely a year, we might almost say scarcely a term, is thus unmarked during our past history.

The links which thus bind man to man in any corporation or fraternity cannot be broken. We may neglect them, forget them, profess to despise them, but they still exist. Nothing can remove that sense of continuity with the past which, on a far wider and more solemn scale, is expressed in the words of the hymn, "Part of the host have crossed the flood, and part are crossing now."

The links of attachment are double: prospective as well as retrospective. If there is the tie of gratitude to the past there is also that of obligation to the future.

You remember Robert Browning's reflections at the sight of Trafalgar and Cape St. Vincent: "Here and here did England help me; how can I help England, say?"

It is but one here and there who can feel

himself called on to take a place in our roll-call.
But remember this. The aggregate of those
benefactions, as we have seen, is made up not so
much by a few great gifts as by innumerable
small ones, significant rather as tokens of kindly
will than for what they might fetch in the
market. May we not say that the aggregate of
acknowledgment for them is similarly to be
sought, not in costly return gifts, but in the
numberless petty acts of daily life which lie in
the power of us all; in the effort to use to the
utmost the privileges now before us; the
determination that a mere grasping after
prizes shall not get the upper hand; a
resolution that no act or neglect of ours
shall soil the fair fame of the ancient house; a
continued effort to smooth the path of others
and to help them on their way? So shall we
"fruitfully use those temporal things" which
men of the past "charitably bestowed for our
comfort."

V.

PRE-REFORMATION COLLEGE LIFE.

(Being a Paper read to the Caius Historical Society.)

What I propose to do to-night is to give you some account of College life as it was 400 years ago. I fear, however, that there is not very much to be said on this subject. We are looking down a long cavernous passage, where the light is feeble, and the outlines soon become dim and uncertain. But the subject ought to be one of some interest to you of the present day, for the men of whom I shall speak are your predecessors, bound to you by a chain in which, however long, no single link is missing. That is a rather startling fact when we come to reflect upon it. Every one of you is in intimate personal relation with some of those who belong to the year before you. So were they with those who preceded them. And thus we may go back step by step, to the very origin of the Foundation. Fortunately for our country there has been no breach of continuity by war, nor even by plague. Till quite recent times I doubt if there was ever a single day, from year's end to year's end, in which some fellows and scholars were not in residence, and therefore in personal communication.

To begin. There is one natural prejudice which you have to overcome. Those who are familiar with the social prestige and intellectual claims of any one of our more important colleges in the present day, may find it difficult to realize what relatively humble institutions they were 400 years ago. As corporations owning land, and making an architectural display, they were dwarfed into insignificance by the local monasteries. The Prior of Barnwell, with his grand church, stately buildings, numerous retinue, and ecclesiastical pomp, must have looked down from a very lordly height upon any master of a college of his own day. And, besides Barnwell, there were the three great foundations of the Friars: the Franciscans, the Dominicans, and the Augustinians. The former of these, as is well known, had such a magnificent church that the University made an earnest attempt, unfortunately in vain, to secure it for their own purposes after the Suppression. And even these great local foundations did not belong to the first order, so far as our country is concerned. We are apt to forget what a lofty standard must have been set, by the monasteries all over England, of the dignified display which might be expected in a really great corporation.

But again. It was not only in comparison with the monasteries that the earlier Colleges took a secondary place. There can be little doubt that, even within the University, the Hostels occupied in some respects the primary place in public estimation. At any rate it was in them, rather than in the Colleges, that such

young men of rank and wealth as then
frequented the University were mostly to be
found. If any difficulty is felt in realizing
the exact significance of this state of things,
a parallel can easily be supplied. The
occupants of the Colleges, as compared with
those of the Hostels, corresponded pretty
closely, I apprehend, with the " collegers " as
distinguished from the " oppidans " of one of
our ancient schools. Things have greatly
changed of late years; but older men can
remember the time when a very distinct tone
of social superiority was assumed by the latter
over the former. What may be called the
statutable precedence, consisting in being on
the foundation, may easily be superseded by
the social precedence arising out of rank and
wealth.

Suppose then that we were to pay a visit
to one of our ancient Colleges, what should
we find? In the first place, it may be
remarked that some search would probably
be required before the College was discovered.
Even within the memory of living men it
would have been almost possible for anyone
to walk from where the Fitzwilliam stands to
St. Sepulchre's Church, without catching sight
of any College at all, except Pembroke. There
was once a high wall in front of Peterhouse.
Corpus was accessible or visible only by a passage
past St. Bene't's Church. What is now King's
Parade was a narrow street of lofty old houses,
from the top stories of which, it used to be
said, people might almost have shaken hands.

High walls in front of Trinity and St. John's
hid most of their buildings except the gate-
ways. And in earlier times the Colleges were
even more closely packed away behind the
houses of the town. Suppose yourself standing
in front of St. Mary's with your back to the
church, and try to picture the scene that
would meet the eye. In front, and to right
and left, extends uninterruptedly a row of
dwellings, of which perhaps a still existent old
building here and there, such as Buol's present
restaurant, or the Oriental Café, might be a
favourable specimen. Over the chimney tops,
possibly, a glimpse might be caught of the
turrets of King's Chapel, then just completed;
but hardly any other sign of College or University buildings would be detected. If you
look at Hamond's Map of Cambridge of 1590,
of which a copy hangs on the staircase of the
University Library, you will easily understand
all this. But you must remember that this
map displays one great improvement which was
then quite recent. This was the so-called
"University Street" due to the liberality of
Archbishop Parker; a passage cleared through
the houses in front and leading directly to the
Public Schools.

To get to Gonville Hall, you would go a
little further along the main street, past where
our Gate of Humility stands, and turn down
Findsilver Lane—Trinity Lane as we now call
it—which, also, was hedged in by houses on
each side. Picking your way through the filth
you would have to walk carefully; for the lane

bore a bad reputation, and was commonly called by a name too course to repeat. In fact at one time a Royal Injunction had been directed to the masters of Gonville Hall and Michael House, the two houses which faced each other there. It stated that such a "horror abominabilis" encountered the students on their way thereby to the Schools, owing to the state of the drains— open gutters presumably—that the authorities were to put them in order at once. "Otherwise," it went on to say, in language whose vigour the modern sufferer from such nuisances might wish to see revived, "we shall provide another and more severe remedy for you and for them." And this dirty lane was one of the principal thoroughfares of the town. It provided practically the only access to the Schools and Library; to King's College, Clare, Trinity Hall, Gonville and Michael House, as well as to several of the larger hostels.

Half way down this lane you would come upon a couple of ancient buildings to the left, with a small gateway between them. This was the whole of the show which our College had to make outside. These old buildings were already somewhat decayed, for they represented the nucleus of the original College. They were the houses bought by Gonville's executor when the foundation was placed on its present site in 1353. Entering by the small gateway, the only means of access, we should find ourselves in the present Gonville Court, which then constituted the entire College. Any modern occupant would recognise it. In front, as you enter, stands the

Chapel; essentially the present building, though its red brick surface was not faced with masonry as now. To the right of this stands the Master's chamber. This latter occupied the site of the present passage-way between the first two courts, and also included the entrance porch of the present Lodge. To the right stand the Library and Hall. Here, again, the ancient erection of brick and clunch is mostly still standing, though concealed by its eighteenth century coating of ashlar. The square windows which now replace the ancient narrow lights, give it of course a very modern look. To the left is a block of students' chambers, of which however no trace is left in the existing edifice. These were the buildings erected by the liberality of Lady Elizabeth Clere, and at the time in question they were quite new. Like nearly all else in the Court, these buildings would be constructed with the old red brick, mixed perhaps with the common clunch. Stone, as you know, was a very rare material in Cambridge. The so-called " Stone-house," the nucleus of the original College, was quite an exception; it acquired its name because its materials were unusual. It was probably somewhat in the style of the well-known " Pythagoras Hall," the ancient Norman house at the back of St. John's College.

So much for the material fabric. What is there to be said about the personal element? The Master at the time was Dr. Buckenham, a man of some mark and influence in the University. As Vice-Chancellor he was active

and efficient. He compiled a list of charters and
other documents, known at the Registry as the
"Old Black Book." He also took part in an
important arbitration between the University
and the Prior of Barnwell. That he was a man
of personal influence may be concluded from
the variety of gifts and bequests which accrued
to the College during his time. The east side of
the Court, as I have just said, was completed.
The Elie Almshouses, still connected with the
College, came into our patronage about the
same time. In fact Buckenham seems to have
been one of those very useful men who, though
not themselves rich, seem to possess the knack
of securing a good deal of help from those who
are rich. One wealthy Norwich merchant gave
us the chantry of St. Michael's Coslany. Another
presented a bell for the Chapel : it was afterwards exchanged as being too big, but I have
no doubt that our monkish residents, when
they heard its tinkle, must have smiled in pity
as they thought of their own numerous and
deep-toned bells. The quaintest of these gifts
deserves closer description. It came from one
of the well-known Lestrange family of Norfolk
and consisted of "seven score ewes and three
score lambs," "to be delyvered to the sayde
master and felowes at midsomer." The College
in return—we have the deed in our Treasury—
binds itself, under its common seal, to pray for
the soul of John Lestrange himself as well as
for those of "his wyffe, his fathere and mothere,
his both brothers, his father yn lawe Thomas
Lestrange esquyer, and for the soul of all his

benefactors and all good Crysten soules." Dr. Caius tells us that the sheep were sold—very naturally, as we had no convenient land on which to pasture them.

Several of the fellows and scholars of the time were also men of either mark or promise. In fact, if we take into account not actual, but proportional, numbers, it may be doubted if the College has ever more completely fulfilled the ideal, entertained by the various founders. (The principal members here referred to are recorded in the previous essay.)

Now whatever views may be entertained as to the primary duty of encouraging scientific research and scholarship, and carrying on the instruction of the young, there can be little doubt as to what was the intention of most of our original founders. Rightly or wrongly, what they desired was that the recipient of their bounty should lay a solid foundation by study here, and then go out into the world for the service of the Church and State. If we compare what was thus achieved by the men of 1520 with the corresponding performances of their successors from two to three centuries afterwards, the contrast presented is not so entirely in favour of the later date as those who represent it might wish to believe.

But what have we to say, it may be asked, about those who were not members of the foundation: about "the ordinary students," in the language of the present day. They certainly did come into residence, though not in large numbers: to what classes of society did they belong? In the case of most of our Colleges it is impossible to ascertain anything definite on this point. There was no system of matriculation till long afterwards, and anything in the way of College Admission Registers was then quite unknown. Our own register,—due to the foresight of Dr. Caius,—does not begin till 1560. When students from the outside did come into residence in a college they seem just to have settled their accounts with the steward, or in later days with their tutor, by some private arrangement. No reference to their presence is made in the regular College accounts.

Fortunately for us, as it so happens, our own College books supply an exception to this almost universal blank. For a number of years, especially towards the beginning of the sixteenth century, a list of names is given at the end of each half-year's accounts, headed *Pensionarii*: that is, it comprises the men who paid for their board and lodging. It is merely a list of surnames, as it stands, and needs a good deal of interpretation; but by reference to the University Grace books, and various other sources of information, we can recover a number of facts about the majority of those who are thus recorded. So far as I know, this inlet into the past history of University life is almost unique.

It will perhaps surprise you to know that the most important constituent, numerically, consisted of *monks*. College life was, of course, a mere episode, and a brief one, in their career;

E

and careful precautions were taken to prevent
the comparatively secular life in the University
from alienating their thoughts from their lifelong service. As I have elsewhere given a
detailed account of this element in College life
—(see the following essay)—no more need be
said on this head, beyond the fact that these
visitors formed a decided majority of the
occasional students. Those at Gonville Hall
came mostly from the Benedictine Monastery
at Norwich; from the splendid Cluniac Priory
at Lewes; and from the House of the Augustinian Canons at Westacre in Norfolk.

The next constituent element consisted of
parochial clergy. This, again, may cause surprise, for to most people it will seem rather an
inversion of the natural course of things that
men should come to College after, instead of
before, their ordination. But we must remember that in those days an extremely small
proportion of the parochial clergy, especially in
the rural districts, were University graduates.
It was not until after the Reformation that the
helps to poor students, in the shape of 'bible-
clerkships'—scholarships as we now call them
—sizarships and so forth, came to be generally
introduced. In Gonville Hall, for instance, in
1520, there were only three scholarships in
existence, and all these were then of quite
recent introduction.

From a very early date a certain number of
the beneficed clergy had come to feel a wish for
study in College, for a degree, and for whatever
professional advancement might follow from a

degree. They consequently applied to their bishop for permission to leave their cure for two or three years in order to study at Cambridge or Oxford. Anyone who consults the Bishops' registers and Act Books will find there a number of such licences for non-residence for the avowed purpose of study. Sometimes these parish priests appealed to the Pope ; for similar permissions are to be found among the Papal Letters, of which several volumes have been published. I will give a single instance, of early date, as it is one of special interest to us. In October 1405, a papal dispensation was granted to Thomas Aylward, vicar of Havant in Hants., allowing him to let the fruits of his benefice for five years, whilst studying at a University. Now it was this Thomas Aylward, as Caius tells us in his *Annals*, who founded what was called a "chest,"—that is, a small lending bank—for poor students at Gonville Hall. Such benefactions were not uncommon in those times. We have no documentary evidence as to where he went for his studies, but I should think there can be little doubt that it was in Gonville Hall that Aylward came to reside, and that his keen realisation of the difficulties and hardships of the poorer students had prompted him to show his gratitude in this substantial way.

As the Reformation drew near, this class of residents became somewhat more numerous, and a fair proportion of them are to be found amongst our pensioners. Some of these belong to the same class as Aylward ; that is, they were comparatively wealthy or well-born. For instance, one or two members of the De La Pole family, sons of the Duke of Suffolk, were pensioners at this time. Humphrey Pole, in fact, found life so pleasant here that he stayed on apparently for some 15 years, though he held preferment elsewhere. So, seemingly, did William Boleyn, an uncle of the unfortunate Queen of Henry VIII., for we find him in residence here for many years after his M.A. degree. These men rented good chambers, and evidently made themselves thoroughly comfortable during their College life.

But besides these rich and well-connected priests, there were not a few from the ranks of the ordinary parochial clergy. Their appearance in the University at this period was doubtless closely connected, partly as cause, partly as effect, with the religious upheaval of the Reformation. No district could be so remote but what the leaven of the Reformation was beginning to work in it. There must have been many country parishes where the parson was anxious to learn something about the new views. A typical illustration of this class is afforded by Thomas Patmore, rector of Much Hadham, Herts., who resided in the College for some two years about this time. Foxe, in his *Book of Martyrs*, has something to say about him, as he was deprived of his living for his opinions, and imprisoned for two years in the Lollards' Tower at Lambeth. Side by side with him might have been seen Sygar Nicholson, well-known as the University printer, and also

as a sufferer for his religious opinions. As
Latimer indignantly remarked, some years
later, when addressing one of the persecutors:
"Do you not hold Nicholson, Smyth—(this was
Simon Smith, a fellow of Gonville Hall)—
Patmore, with many others, in prison at this
hour?"

Besides the clergy, regular and secular, a few
others would also be found who belonged to
a class of society more commonly found in
College to-day. That is, there would be some
whose parents were in easy circumstances or
who belonged to the professional classes. As a
rule such men were rather rare visitors in the
Colleges, but their names are now and then to
be found on our lists. Thus, there can be little
doubt that the "Her," who is entered amongst
the pensioners of 1509, may be identified with
the Nicholas Hare, afterwards M.P. for Norfolk,
Speaker of the House of Commons, and Master
of the Rolls. And we know that a few years
later, Thomas Gresham, the famous merchant
and founder of the Royal Exchange, was
similarly a resident. For a long time this fact
only rested on the testimony of his friend and
contemporary, John Caius, but we have since
found the name recorded as a pensioner in the
bursar's accounts.

It is a strange picture that thus rises up
before us when we try to realise what was the
state of the society in College at the time.
They must have met together every day,
especially in Hall and in Chapel. Fancy an
assembly, of some 25 or 30 men altogether,

gathered round the table at meal times ; in that same building which we have just recently restored as an annexe to the Library. It was a critical period, when religious passions were strongly excited, and when the merest utterance of a wrong opinion might at any moment lead to imprisonment if not to death. One of the charges against Patmore, whom I have just mentioned, was that, when at Cambridge he had once declared that "he did not set a bottle of hay by the Pope's curse." One cannot but wonder whether this remark was a retort hurled across the table at one or other of the monks who were sitting there with him. In after life these old College pensioners must have sometimes met again : perhaps on opposite sides, or after wide changes of opinion. Peter Valentius, for instance, was a resident in 1521. He had already distinguished himself by his reforming zeal, and by a bold attack on the Proclamation of Indulgences. After the example of Luther, he posted a defiant notice on the copy affixed against the gate of the Schools at Cambridge. Foxe records a visit Valentius paid to two of the Marian martyrs, shortly before their death. Of the members of the Commission who condemned these men two bear names known in the College, and may well have been personally familiar to Valentius. These were Shaxton, who had been a resident fellow in 1520, and Robert Steward. Steward resided as a pensioner for several years about the same time. He was subsequently Prior of the Monastery at Ely, and after the Suppression

became the first dean of the Cathedral. Thomas
Bacon, a fellow in 1521, and afterwards Master
of the College, was also present at the death of
these two martyrs.

As to the daily life of these ancient residents,
it need hardly be said that this would seem
terribly monotonous and severe to modern
apprehension. The Chapel service was at 5 a.m.
in Dr. Caius' time, and we may be quite sure
that it was not later than this a generation
before. Every resident, of course, had to
attend; Bishop Bateman, in his statutes, had
laid down stringent regulations on this point.
It may be remarked that the importance of the
College Chapel, in the daily routine of life, had
been gradually increased. At the outset, the
building was only to be used as an "oratory,"
for family prayers, as we should now say. For
daily attendance at mass, and for all the more
solemn ceremonies, the students had to attend
at the parish church, St. Michael's. By a suc-
cession of Papal and Episcopal concessions, the
privileges of the College had been gradually
extended. The last of these was a bull of
Alexander VI., which granted permission to the
Master and Fellows to reserve the Sacrament,
and to bury their dead within our walls. This
was in 1500, and, as far as we know, advantage
seems speedily to have been taken of the last
permission. The brass still remains which
records the burial of Walter Stubbe, brother of
a Master of the College, in 1514. There is, as
you know, another brass, of much the same
date, to some unknown man in plate armour.

The coats of arms, which would have served to identify him, have unfortunately disappeared ; so we are unable to say whether he was one of our pensioners. But it is hardly likely that any one would be buried there who was not at the time a resident in College.

Though the number of attendants at worship was not large, the services were probably—in accordance with pre-Reformation practice—of a somewhat ornate kind, at least on the greater festivals. The College possessed many vestments and other ornaments. In fact Dr. Caius tells us that, in his day, "the precious vestments of white linen embroidered with gold," which were amongst the original gifts of Bishop Bateman, were actually still in use on the more solemn festivals of the Virgin. If any of you had the opportunity of visiting the loan collection at the Church Congress at Cambridge, you can judge how elaborate and splendid such things could be in medieval days.

As to the vessels, or the most part of them, we know the subsequent fate. When the permissible ornaments were restricted by law, Dr. Caius seems to have saved as many of the old ones as he could, and to have preserved them in his chambers. These were routed out by the Fellows shortly before his death, and destroyed, with much glee, in a bonfire in the court. The Vice-Chancellor, Dr. Byng, reports the transaction to the Chancellor, with evident satisfaction, and described the destruction of what he calls the "Popish Trumpery." The list included "vestments, albs, tunicles, stoles,

manicles, corporos clothes, with the pix and
sindon, and canopy, besides holy water stoups,
with sprinkles, pax, sensars, superalteries,
tables of idolls, masse books, portuises and
grailles, with other such stuffe as might have
furnished divers massers at one instant ":—a
small Art collection in itself. They burnt what
they could and smashed up the rest. So the
new treated the old !

It need hardly be said that a small society,
consisting of such elements as I have described
above, was necessarily of a somewhat studious
and quiet character. Much of their time was
probably spent in the College Library. In fact
the opportunity of using the library would be
one of the main inducements to a residence in
College. In days when students were mostly
very poor, and books were mostly very scarce
and dear; and when moreover the student had
to go to the books, instead of expecting the books
to come to him, the help afforded by a good
library would be invaluable. The bulk of the
volumes would of course still be in MS., and it
need hardly be said that they were all carefully
chained to their shelves.

That ancient library, as most of you know,
still exists, having been recently restored and
converted into a second Combination room.
The walls are in large part the ancient walls,
and the roof contains the ancient timber beams.
The windows on the inner side were walled in
long ago, and those looking towards the court
were enlarged. The glass which once adorned
them had been the gift of, and still recalled the

names of, some famous old scholars and prelates. Amongst these was William Lyndwood, Bishop of St. David's, a notable writer on the Canon Law. Not a little of his work had probably been done there, before those shelves, in the days when he was a student here. Our library, thanks partly to Bateman, was rather strong in that department.

One would like to have a true picture of that library as it once was :—to try to recognize some of the few students who might have been found there, say on some dull day in winter, in the dimly lighted building—it was of course entirely unwarmed — as with numbed fingers they handled the iron chains which secured the precious volumes. They are probably working up some question which has to be keenly discussed at the next "opposition" or "reponsion" in the Schools, when they stand for the Civil or Canon Law degree. Or they may be preparing for their next sermon *ad clerum* in St. Mary's or *ad populum* at St. Paul's Cross, if Theology be their faculty. It may be remarked that, so far as the College was concerned, all their work had to be done by themselves, as there were no lecturers or tutors in existence yet. They occupied very much the same position, in fact, as those whom we now term "Advanced or Research" students : — (no enquirer into the past will be surprised at finding that some vaunted modern improvement is really little more than a re-introduction of customs familiar centuries ago). They already knew something of their subject; and were attracted, partly by the

society of learned men, but mainly by the local
advantages for study. Their actual work had to
be carried on mostly on their own initiative,
and, of course, the Library corresponded somewhat to the modern Laboratory.

If we were to follow them into the Dining
Hall we should again find the life simple and
severe. Here, also, recent and successful restoration will enable you to some extent to recall the
past; for the ancient Hall has just been put
back, as nearly as possible, into its old form; the
floor was of stone, covered in the usual way with
rushes. The walls were bare, in all likelihood;
and, as Dr. Caius tells us, no attempt was yet
made to warm it even in the depth of winter.
In fact, these latter alleviations were at the
prompting and bequest of Bishop Shaxton,
already referred to as a Resident Fellow at the
time. He it was, who—doubtless keenly mindful
of what he himself had once undergone in the
days when he was a poor bible-clerk—combined
with one or two other generous men to provide a
brazier to stand in the Hall. He also furnished
a supply of charcoal for it, but this only for the
three months from All Saints' day to the 2nd of
February. This was first started in 1565. It
shows how what are now considered the barest
necessaries for the poor were once the coveted
luxuries of the comparatively well-to-do, that
this gift was to be nightly celebrated by a psalm
of thanksgiving. Those who were not present
at this were to have no place near the fire.
It was Shaxton, too, who bequeathed some
"hangings," tapestry presumably, to cover the

nakedness of the bare walls; and who, remember-
ing what was the ordinary fare at table, left
a sum of money wherewith, as he phrased it, "to
solace the company at Christmas."

If we could watch this company at meal-time,
we should probably see them all sitting together
at one table; for the elaborate distinctions of
fellow-commoners, pensioners, and so forth,
were seemingly an introduction of later days.
The Master of course was always present.
Scarcely any food was allowed to be taken in
College except in common at the public table.
At the time in question the dinner hour was
probably about 10 and the supper about 5.

The whole assembly might perhaps number
about 25 or 30 at most; nearly half of these, as I
have already said, consisting of monks, whom
we can figure dressed in the distinctive garb of
their various Orders. The ordinary fare at table
was very plain. A bible-clerk would be reading
the lessons or some religious work. This was
an office of recent introduction in our College,
the bible-clerk being what would now be called
a scholar. By Bateman's statutes silence was
commanded at table; a Fellow was to read the
scriptures; and when there was any talk in the
College it was always to be in Latin. To the
professional student, especially if, as was not
unfrequently the case, he had studied at foreign
Universities, this last condition would be no
burden. Erasmus, I suppose, was just as glib in
Latin as in his native Dutch. But we can
hardly suppose that the country clergyman or
the miscellaneous "pensioner" found such a

regulation easy of acceptance. It does not need much knowledge of human nature to guess that the practical result was very much what it was in girls' schools of a generation or two ago, when the pupils were forbidden to speak to each other in any language but French. Such waiting as was required was presumably performed by poor students, who afterwards sat down at the table and finished what was left. This was certainly so a little later, when they were called sizars.

But had these men any "amusements"? I am afraid that, in the current sense of the term, they had to go without them. Of course no gathering of Englishmen, which included young men of family and wealth, could fail to furnish those who wanted to indulge in the amusements of their class; in hawking, hunting, and so forth. I need hardly say that Cambridge in those days offered magnificent opportunities for such sport, as indeed it continued to do for centuries afterwards. There was the limitless range of the Fens to the north; a wide extent of entirely unenclosed land round about the town; and all the open down country towards Newmarket, which offered such attractions to James I. a century later. But the few University students who could indulge in such pursuits would probably be found in a Hostel rather than in a College. It is a significant fact that whereas Caius, compiling his statutes some 30 or 40 years later, thought it necessary peremptorily to forbid every such kind of unscholarly pursuit, Bateman, our earlier legislator, did not think it needful to refer to the subject in any way.

Caius, for instance, forbids the students to keep "fierce birds," presumably falcons and hawks. This, of course, was in the Elizabethan days, when young men of family were beginning to flock to the Colleges.

As to games, properly so called, I have spoken more fully elsewhere (see essay VI.). I will only say now that Football, at any rate, was probably already a popular amusement amongst the younger students. It certainly was so a generation later. Here, again, we have the evidence of Dr. Caius' prohibitions. He absolutely forbids what would be called "Inter-collegiate" play, and confines the game to the College precincts. Were they, I wonder, to kick the ball about in the College court? There was nowhere else, for they can hardly have been suffered in the Master's or Fellows' gardens.

If we may trust the account which Caius himself gives of the habits of the youths of his own day—he "came up" in 1529—one would almost suppose that their sole diversion and main occupation was found in attendance on the public disputations in the Schools: that they spent their time in preparation for their own performances there, when they came to graduate, and in critical observation of the performances of their companions. If any relaxation from such a strenuous occupation was needed it was found in the amusement provided by the preparation for, and performance of, a Latin play during the Christmas holidays. When an old man lapses into the retrospective vein and begins to contrast the present with the

past, we naturally feel inclined to take a
certain discount off the comparative estimate
which he offers. But after all due allowance
has been made, there can be little doubt that
these discussions played a really important part
in the life of such students as we are considering.
The inmates of a College were, as I have said,
somewhat of a picked class. They had mostly
come here with a view to professional advancement, and skill in academic exercises would be
an important element in professional success.
There was no such thing then, remember, as
the Union or a Debating Society. If a man of
ready wit and fluent speech wished to display
his powers, and to win a public triumph over
his opponents, this was his only opportunity of
doing so. Even in the eighteenth century, when
the Mathematical Tripos was beginning to domin-
ate, considerable interest was still felt in the
School disputes. A brilliant attack or defence
probably attracted the same sort of notice as would
an unusually good speech at the Union now.

That there was also a rowdy element in the
University even in his own day, Dr. Caius
admits, and he has given a description of what
in modern language would be called a "rag,"
which occurred just before his own time. Need
I say that he assures us that the miscreants
came from outside, and that the members of
his own Hall were passive victims ? He has
recorded the event in his *Annals.* He says that
in 1521 one of those frequent disputes between
the "Northern" and "Southern" factions in
the University assumed the form of a serious

riot. The Gonville men mostly belonged to the latter side; that is, were born south of the Trent; but the former faction was very strong in Cambridge, Yorkshire men, in particular, being always numerous. The students at Gerard's Hostel, on the other side of the road,—mostly northerners,—in their general animosity against their neighbours, and harbouring special spite against Humphrey De La Pole, as a prominent southerner (so Caius tells us), made an organized attack on Gonville Hall. They set fire to the entrance gate, "rushed" the College, invaded the kitchen and buttery, spilt all the liquor they could find, and would— but for the promptitude of the butler, who hid the silver vessels and other articles of value in the College well—have plundered the place. It is a curious illustration of the bitterness of these party divisions, that we are assured that the assault was encouraged by the Vice-Chancellor, a northerner by origin, though he pretended to dissuade his party from any display of violence. ("Ad quod facinus tacito nutu provocabat Johannes Stachouse, ejus anni procancellarius, homo ejusdem gentis et factionis; verbo tamen dissuadebat.") William Tayte, the principal of Gerard's Hostel—he had been proctor 20 years before—was, we are told, the main contriver of the outrage. According to Caius, Tayte came in the end to feel some penitence for what he had done, and shortly before his death gave a number of books to the Library. But his name still stands in the *Annals* as one of our *malefactors*.

VI.

MONKS IN COLLEGE.

About the time, towards the middle fifties,
when the country at large was beginning to
feel a revived interest in the constitution and
condition of the old Universities, and was
coming to the decided conclusion that they
stood in need of some reformation, few complaints were commoner than that which was
directed against the so-called "*monkish*"
character and position of the college Fellow.
The resemblance was a rather superficial one,
for the essence of the religious life lay in its
incessant devotion, not to study, but to prayer
and praise; and in its perpetual enforcement
of these duties, under the triple vow of chastity,
poverty and obedience. It would have been a
strange sort of monastery in which the abbot
was generally married, and which any monk
might quit at once, in case he should feel
inclined to go out into the world; and where,
moreover, each brother had at least one or two
rooms for his own private use, and could spend
his time just as he pleased. It is no doubt
true that if we go some centuries back this
contrast becomes less striking. Though there
was not in general, strictly speaking, any vow
of obedience to the Head on the part of the
Fellow, it is certain that the Master possessed,
and often exercised, a considerable amount of
autocratic power; a power the exercise of which

would have startled the whole house a couple of centuries later. Moreover, the *common*, as distinguished from the individual life, was a much more prominent and permanent characteristic in early times. Attendance at the college chapel was compulsory twice daily, and the meals were taken in common—there are, for instance, stringent regulations in the statutes of Dr. Caius as to the amount of food which the fellows might have in private, in their own rooms. Though there was never, I believe, a common dormitory in colleges, it is well known that privacy, in the modern sense, was quite out of the question. Exigencies of economy rendered this impossible; for neither space nor money could be afforded to lodge each man separately, even if the extreme youth of the scholars had made this desirable. These, however, were recognised characteristics of life in earlier days, and are very far from bringing us back to any form of life so minutely regulated for religious purposes as to entitle it to be called "monkish."

These remarks are intended to be preliminary to a slight sketch of the state of things when real monks actually did reside in our college buildings. That a certain number of them came into residence here and at Oxford, for the purpose of study, in the times before the Reformation, is well known to everyone acquainted with the history of the University. Certain colleges or halls were thus specially frequented by members of this or that religious order—thus Buckingham College, out of which

Magdalene was refounded, was mainly frequented by Benedictine monks; and as we shall presently see, Gonville Hall was a favourite place of resort for Augustinian canons. But, though this general fact has long been familiarly known, nearly all details have been entirely wanting. The fact is that an almost impenetrable cloud of obscurity hangs over the social life and condition of all college students in early days, except those who were actually on the foundation. There was no University Matriculation—at least none is recorded—until 1544. The earliest general College Admission Register—that of Gonville and Caius—does not commence until 1560. It is true that the names of those on the foundation—that is of fellows, scholars and certain college servants—can often be recovered from a very early date, as they are generally recorded in the bursar's account books. But of the class which would now be called pensioners, such as form the bulk of the students of the present day, we know almost nothing whatever. Their very names are totally lost, except where, now and then, owing to their celebrity or to some other cause, their connection with some particular college or hall has been preserved. This is the case, for instance, with Sir Thomas Gresham. There is,[1] I believe, no other evidence of his having been educated at Gonville Hall, than the remark, casually made by Dr. Caius in his *Annals*, that the founder of the Royal Exchange had been

---

[1] Since this was first written Gresham's name has been found in some old account books of the time.

one of his contemporaries here. The early pensioners in fact seem to have been considered as not strictly belonging to the college: not being on the foundation, they were scarcely taken more account of than if they had been " parlour-boarders " at some modern school, and their names are scarcely ever recorded.

There are, however, a few exceptions to this general rule. There is a short period during which a ray of light is let in upon this constituent element of college life. In our earliest *Compotus*, or Bursar's Book, which commences in 1422, and extends (unfortunately with many gaps) to about 1523, there are certain years in which, for some cause, the names of all the *pensionarii* resident in the college at the time are recorded. This is generally the case from 1509 to 1523, for instance, and it is desirable to make the most of the light which is thus afforded. In the half-year's account, made up to Lady Day 1513, we have the following list:—

Ds Humf. de la Pole debet Xii^{li} xvi^s vii^d
Mr Farwell debet xxx^s
Doctor Wyght xx^s
Mr Harman iii^s iv^d
Mr Reppys, monachus, debet pro sua pensione i^s viii^d
Monachi Norwicenses debent xiiii^s
Ds Belham debet iii^s iv^d
Ds Mayner debet iii^s iv^d
Ds Brycotte debet iii^s
Mr Englysthe debet xxx^s
Mr Carman debet vi^s viii^d

Mr Bolen debet vi^s viii^d
Mr Knyvett debet vi^s viii^d
Monachi de Lewse debent x^s
Ds Atherole et D^s Crome debent pro 3
terminis x^s
Mr Aldrych debet v^s
These, with the Master, seven Fellows and
three scholars, make up apparently the entire
resident body of the college at the time; so
that, numerically, these pensioners were an
important element in the constitution of the
society. The youth who heads the list, De la
Pole, as a son of the Duke of Suffolk, stands
of course in a class by himself, and doubtless
paid a fancy price for his lodging and board.
He is, I think, the only one in the list who at
all corresponds to the fellow-commoners of
later times; to those, that is, who came here,
as youths of family, not primarily for the
purpose of professional study or to obtain a
degree, but rather for such general culture as
residence here might be hoped to encourage.
Two or three of the remainder are Masters of
Arts, probably staying on with a view of
securing the higher degrees of Doctor in
Theology, Civil or Canon Law, or Medicine.
The rest are mainly monks; and it is to them
that I want to call attention, as it shews how
in a small college—and Gonville Hall was then
one of the smallest in Cambridge—a considerable number of students were sent up by their
respective monasteries. Some, it will be seen,
are specifically described as being monks in the
above list; in the case of others, we find their

names recurring in subsequent years under similar designations. Mayner, for instance, resided for six or seven years, and is generally described as canonicus; *i.e.* he was presumably an Augustinian canon from Westacre, in Norfolk. Brycotte belonged to the same Order. The above list, as it stands, may seem little more than a mere string of names; but it acquires a very different significance when we study it in the light of the information yielded by the Visitation of the Norfolk and Suffolk monasteries. Some of the greater houses secured papal exemption from all control of this kind, but the others were duly subject to regular episcopal Visitation; and the results of some of these Visitations have been preserved.[1] They contain reports of the inspection, by the Bishop of Norwich, of all the religious houses in his diocese which were not exempt from his jurisdiction. The earliest Visitation of those which are thus recorded is in 1494, the latest in 1532:— on the very eve of the Suppression. The reports are mainly made up of statements of breaches of discipline, for the most part of a trifling character, given by the priors and others in authority. They also contain complaints, by the monks, of curtailments of their privileges, and such other matters.

What concerns us here, however, are the references which they contain to University life and study. In one religious house after another we find it noted that a monk is absent at the

---

[1] They were published by Dr. Jessopp for the Camden Society, No. XLIII.

University, in pursuit of his studies; or if he could not be sent there, it is complained that the due provision for his support at College had been withheld. Many of the monasteries were too small or too poor to be able thus to support students at a distance; but such houses as the great Benedictine Priory at Norwich, and the Augustinian Priory at Westacre, seem generally to have had two or three at least of their younger members in training at Cambridge. This was especially the case with Westacre, a house which, as Dr. Jessopp tells us, was much favoured by the sons of the Norfolk gentry, and in which several of the names from the above list may be found. Where the monastery was too poor to support a student out of its corporate funds, he was sometimes sent at the expense of his own friends. Thus in Butley, in 1514, a small house in debt at the time, we are told that "Thomas Orford est bonus grammatista et deditus litteris, et amici volunt exhibere[1] eum in Universitate sumptibus suis." The Bishop directs that this should be done. In 1526 their income had improved, and the Bishop gave orders "quod exhibeatur scholaris in Universitate sumptibus domus." At Norwich, in 1532, three or four of the monks complain, "quod scholares non exhibentur more solito:"— "conqueritur de scholaribus non exhibitis more solito in Universitate." At Westacre in 1520

---

[1] *"Exhibere"* was the technical term for supporting a scholar at the University: *exhibitio* being the name for the stipend. The popular distinction between a scholarship and an exhibition was of much later date.

the number of the resident canons is short,
"quia tres in Universitate," and so on.

But to come to details in respect of some
of the men in our list above. In the visitation
of Westacre in 1520, Magister Mayner, Canon
of the Priory, is described as "idoneus preceptor
pro confratribus." He had then just returned
from college, where he seems to have spent
about seven years in study, and to have finally
graduated as Bachelor in Divinity. His name
recurs at the same Priory in 1526. Thomas
Brycotte, or Byrkhed, who appears as a
pensioner in our books from 1514 to 1523,
where he is generally described as *canonicus*,
states at the Visitation of 1520 that "propter
ejus absentiam in studio, non novit statum
domus:" he had only recently returned from
college. "Belham" is, I apprehend, the same
as Robert Bekham, who appears with Mayner
in the Visitation of Westacre in 1514, when he
complains of his exhibition being insufficiently
paid: "ipse deponens studiens Cantabrigiæ
percepisset pro uno anno viii Marcas pro victu
et vestitu suis, et quod recepit nisi xls." William
Reppes, or Rugg, whose name is on our list, is a
man of some note, as he afterwards became
Bishop of Norwich. He was a Benedictine of
Norwich Priory, and is mentioned in each of
the Visitations of 1514, 1520 and 1526. In 1514
he was sacristan and was selected to preach
the sermon on the occasion of the Bishop's
visit. In 1520 he is described as prior of the
cell, or dependent house, at Yarmouth. In
1526 he was sub-prior at Norwich, on which

occasion a scandal is charged against him by one of his brethren. He became Bishop of Norwich in 1536.

It will be noticed that the residence of monks from Lewes Priory, in Sussex, is recorded above; and this is repeated in several following years. At first sight this seem a departure from the otherwise almost uniformly East Anglian character of the college; but it is probable that county connections and associations had, as usual, something to do with the presence of these visitors. The great priory of St. Pancras at Lewes was a considerable landowner in Norfolk; and, as a matter of fact, the college still holds lands in that county which were purchased from the monks in the fourteenth century. So little is known however of the occupants of the monastery at this particular time that we have no means of identifying the individuals referred to in our list. In the years 1521-3 the Bursar's accounts include, amongst the pensioners, the Prior of Horton. There can scarcely be any doubt that this is Horton in Kent, which was a dependency of Lewes. If so, the person in question was probably Richard Gloucester, alias Brisley, the last Prior of the house, who surrendered it to Henry VIII. a few years later.

If it be asked what were the reasons which induced these monks to come to college, the reply must be that the attractions were very much the same as those which have brought most other students here during the centuries which have elapsed since then. Here and there

the dominant motive may have been sheer love
of speculative study, but the bulk of students
were doubtless attracted by hopes of professional advancement. Then, as 400 years later,
an academic degree had a market value. Even
the inferior degrees, and the training which led
up to them, served to qualify the young monk,
on his return to his house, to act as a teacher
of the novices, and thus to better his position.
We are told of Mayner, after he had left college,
that he was "idoneus preceptor pro confratribus"; and similar reports are given of others.
The superior degrees were still more important
for advancement in the Church. The Doctor of
Divinity, and, even more, he who had devoted
himself to the Canon or Civil Law, had openings
before him in the business of the State at home,
and in political missions abroad, which made it
amply worth his while, on merely professional
grounds, to devote himself to the requisite years
of study. It is often forgotten what a large
amount of important work must often have
been thrown upon the abbots and priors of the
greater Monasteries. At home there were privileges to be secured or regained, and attacks to
be warded off, which must have involved them
in transactions with the Bishop, the Archbishop
or the Courts at Westminster. Then, too, there
were frequent appeals to Rome which had to be
personally looked after. And from time to time
the newly chosen prior had himself to go to
headquarters in order to make his election
good. For all these purposes some knowledge
of the Canon and Civil Law must have been

essential. Bishop Bateman, when he founded Trinity Hall, knew enough of the courts at Rome and Avignon to be aware of this. His object was to secure that some of the secular clergy, as well as the regulars, should be versed in this essential science. Probably, too, the academic degree, with the comparatively wider training and knowledge of the world which it involved, counted for something in the selection of an abbot or prior. It is certainly a fact that a very considerable number of the heads of religious houses at the time of the Suppression were graduates of Cambridge or Oxford. Besides one or two of those referred to above, we may mention Steward, the last prior of the house of Ely, and the first dean there after the Suppression, who was a member of our college. With more knowledge we could probably identify others also.

It may be remarked, in passing, that the cause which since the Reformation has been, numerically speaking, far the most influential in supplying our colleges with students—the fact that an academic degree has generally been required by the bishops as a qualification for ordination—was quite inoperative in earlier times. A University training must have been the privilege of a very few comparatively of the parish priests, and was in no sense a requisite for ordination. A study of such lists of ordination as can be found in most of the bishops' registers in pre-Reformation times, shews us that the great majority of those who entered the priesthood, or received the minor orders, came direct from the religious houses. Speaking roughly, it is doubtful if one in ten of those who received Orders from the Bishop of Ely came from any college in Cambridge: they were nearly all furnished by the various monasteries in the diocese and neighbourhood.

Besides inducements of professional advancement, it seems clear that other motives, not altogether unknown in later times, had some influence in attracting the young monk to college. Rigid, monotonous and almost servile, as the modern student would probably find the conditions of his predecessors 400 years ago, the college life must still have been a welcome change of experience to any thoughtful youth from the cloister. We may well suppose, too, that there was something flattering to their sense of self-importance in the knowledge that they had been selected from their brethren in order to be sent up to the great University. Evidently the young men did not think lightly of themselves. For one thing, they probably insisted on *riding* to Cambridge instead of going on foot. Certainly, at some monasteries, candidates for Orders considered it beneath their dignity to tramp it to Norwich for that purpose. Thus at Butley—by no means an important monastery—two of the monks make this a definite subject of complaint : " Confratres transeunt pedestres pro ordinibus recipiendis, in scandalum domus "—" solent exire pedites et non equitare." This was one of the houses which regularly sent students to the University; for many years they had a comfortable room (honesta camera) reserved for them at Gonville Hall. For the credit of the house, too, it was doubtless insisted that their dress and appointments should be quite up to the mark.

Some amusing indications of this feeling may be detected in certain complaints from several of the brethren at Norwich Priory in 1532. They declare, of two of their number, Norwych and Morton—the former of these, by the way, had been a student at Gonville Hall— that their heads had been quite turned by being sent to college: "Dedignantur ceteros confratres, sunt inflati spiritu alti cordis, et indebitantur in Universitate." So, again, at the Benedictine house of Hulme in Norfolk, in 1514, Roger Multon is complained of "quod est inceptor brigarum, et fuit in Cantabrigia per septem annos, et nihil boni fecit." "He did no good there": "he got into debt." There is something strangely modern in the tone of these complaints. One seems to have heard them, from time to time, in the vernacular tongue, from this or that disappointed parent.

Evidently the young man fresh from the University did not treat his seniors with the respect to which they considered that their age entitled them; but there were probably much deeper causes than this to account for the discord. The leaven of the Reformation was at work in Cambridge, and nowhere was the effect more distinctly traceable at this time than in our own College. It was of Gonville Hall that Bishop Nix, of Norwich—the same who con- ducted the Visitations in question—asserted (see

Essay IV.) that "no clerk came from the college but savoured of the frying pan, spake he never so holily." This distinctive religious character was only applicable during a short time, but the young monk who came into residence here during the period with which we have been concerned would have been thrown into social intercourse with such men as Shaxton, Skipp, Crome and Nycholson. The three former were fellows of the college, and the latter a pensioner about this time. Bearing this fact in mind we may accept with some qualification the charges of conceit and insubordination. It is scarcely likely that the young monk who returned to some remote monastery, after several years spent in the society of these men, should fail to find serious causes of difference with those of his brethren who had stayed behind.

With the suppression of the monasteries this state of things passed away, and we can well suppose that the sudden stoppage of what must have been in the aggregate a very considerable source of supply to the Universities should have been seriously felt. On the old system the promising students were selected by their own houses, and supported in college at the corporate expense. As the author of the interesting account[1] of Durham Priory says, "If the master did see that any of them (the novices) were apt to learning, and did apply his book, and had a pregnant wit withal, then the master did let

---

[1] Published by the Surtees Society, 1842. It was written, long after the suppression, by one who had himself been an inmate of the house.

the prior have intelligence. Then, straightway
after, he was sent to Oxford to school, and there
did learn to study Divinity." The scholarships
and sizarships which began to multiply rapidly
soon after the Reformation, and which only
existed previously in very small numbers, were
in great part called for in order to supply the
want created by the destruction of the religious
houses.

VII.

AN ELIZABETHAN EPISODE IN ENGLISH HISTORY.

Much light has recently been thrown upon that eddy in the current of religious thought which is sometimes called the Counter-Reformation, and which was so prominent during the middle and later years of the reign of Elizabeth. The work of Dr. Jessopp, at once learned and deeply interesting, gives, under the title of "One generation of a Norfolk House," a quantity of general historic information, beyond the details concerning the Walpole family. It is to this work, and to the seven bulky volumes of Mr. Foley, which deal with the lives of the earlier English Jesuits, that I was mainly indebted for my first reference to many of the names which follow. The facts however are largely drawn from our College records or from unpublished MS. authority, and ought therefore to have a certain value of their own. What is attempted in the following pages is nothing but a "large scale map" of a very small portion of the province of general English History. They are intended to illustrate the Roman Catholic revival solely as this is displayed in a single College during a few years of Queen Elizabeth's reign.

In order to understand the significance of the details which follow, attention must be

directed first to a few of the national landmarks
of the age and reign. Queen Elizabeth came
to the throne November 17th, 1558, and the
Romish ritual almost immediately became
illegal in England. But, for the first twelve
years or so after this date, there was little
that could in any reasonable sense be called
persecution. In November, 1569, occurred the
Northern rebellion, and a few months afterwards the famous Bull was issued in which
Queen Elizabeth was formally deposed by the
Pope. This marked a crisis; for the English
Government replied by an Act of Parliament
which not only made it treason to introduce
into the realm any Bull from Rome, but
attached the same penalties to any exercise
of his functions by a priest ordained abroad.
As Dr. Jessopp puts it, "any Catholic priest
admitted to his Orders on the other side of
the Channel, and venturing to exercise his
functions in England, did so at the peril of
his life; and whosoever dared to receive absolu-
tion at his hands incurred the same penalty,
with forfeiture of all his worldly goods besides."
Doubtless it was maintained that what the
priest was punished for was his inferred treason
and not his avowed religion, but the fact
remains that the former was simply inferred
from the latter. The mere fact of his appearance in the country rendered him liable to be
drawn, hanged and quartered, and brought a
similar liability upon those who harboured him.
    As regards the corresponding College dates,
Dr. Caius died in July, 1573, and was succeeded

by Dr. Legge, who remained Master for more than thirty years. It was these two men who are primarily responsible for the character of "Papistry" which for a time the College seems to have enjoyed. The charter of foundation, by which Caius was appointed Master, was obtained in Queen Mary's reign, when of course he must have accepted the Romish doctrine, in which he had been brought up. He was not in any way disturbed, like so many of his colleagues, at the turn of the wheel which so speedily followed; but he probably owed his immunity rather to his scientific reputation, and his signal services to the cause of learning by his recent foundation, than to any sympathy on his own part with the reformed faith. He conformed, of course, to the established ritual, but the constantly repeated charges against him are some evidence of the direction in which his inner sympathies lay. Dr. Legge, we must remember, was expressly selected by his predecessor, a fact which in itself would imply some community of belief and feeling, even if we had not the direct testimony of Dr. Sandys, Archbishop of York, to the fact. The Archbishop, in an often-quoted letter to Lord Burleigh, complains that all the popish gentry of Yorkshire were sending their sons to this College, in consequence of the notorious sympathies of its Master and President.

Those who are familiar only with the existent state of things may be prompted to enquire what could be the influence or power of the Master over the opinions of the students?

The reply is that this influence could be considerable, especially at that time. For one thing the Master had the practical, if not legal, appointment of every tutor; and, after the tutor was appointed, he could assign pupils to him at his choice. The doings of Dr. Caius in this way show that his power was pretty nearly arbitrary and supreme, and the Archbishop of York's complaint against his successor, Dr. Legge, tells the same tale: " He setteth sundry of them (the sons of the Catholic gentry) over to one Swayl of the same house," in order to keep them under special influence. Then again the students, especially the Fellow Commoners—and it was to this order that the sons of these country gentry largely belonged—came up at a very early and impressionable age. They lived with their tutor by day and by night, so that instead of modifying their convictions by free intercourse with the various companions whom they met at study and at play, they were mostly under the pressure of one persistent influence. To which we may add that for students from the remoter parts of the country there were but very few vacations, so far as regards absence from College, so that such influence as the tutor could exert would be nearly unbroken.

The College at this time, like the country at large, was rent with religious disputes between the two parties which may be described, after their extreme members, as Puritan and Papist. It is owing to the existence of these disputes, in fact, that much of the information here given, is obtainable; for the former party persisted in making one complaint and appeal to the Visitor after another, against their adversaries, not a few of which complaints are still to be found in the MSS. at the Record Office and British Museum. The Puritan party amongst the Fellows was much the most numerous, in spite of the Master's influence; for no less than seven of the Resident Fellows at this time (1582) signed a series of protests from which the following extracts are taken almost at random (Lansdowne MSS. No. xxxiii.):—

"That St. Quintin (Anselm, son of Gabriel St. Quintin, Esq., of Harpham, Yorks.), Mr. Swale's pupil, did openly call Mr. Nowell dean of St. Paul's a heretic."

"That Dr. Legge had by his importunate labour brought in one Depup to be Fellow; a man notoriously vicious and suspected to be popish, to whom the founder had so great misliking that he gave especial charge that he should never be Fellow."

"That one Osburne (Edward Osburne, mentioned presently) being convicted of Papistry, the Master did not expulse him."

"Five of the Scholars, Mr. Rokewood, Sayer, Flack, Foster, and Barwick, gathered themselves together to consult whether it were lawful for them to dissemble any longer." (We shall see the results of such consultations in the subsequent history of some of these men.)

These statements are supported by a mass of depositions from the Fellows individually.

Thus Mr. John Paman, under date of June 7, 1582, testifies: "that St. Quintin was called before the Master by him and the words being confessed the Master promised due punishment for them, . . . yet this deponent could never yet hear so much as any private correction to be taken for the same." Then comes a complaint against a youth Fingley, of whom more will be said presently, who was suspected to be one of the seminary priests hovering about the place; "he perverted the youth of the house . . . he absented himself from common prayers and sermons in such wise as he could not be drawn unto them by warning and correction often used by this deponent." "That Mr. Stapelton (son of one of the Yorkshire squires already mentioned) was well-known to the Master both to be corrupt in religion, and to have been free of speech therein unto others, and that this deponent had complained unto the Master of the same Stapelton." Of the obnoxious Mr. Depup he declared "that he was popish it is as well-known by the common report that always was of him, as that he was vicious."

From another appeal which follows, signed by the same seven Fellows, it would seem that their opposition to the Master had brought them into some danger:—"Besides our extreme injuries and late intended expulsions we are more and more daily molested and contemned, not only by the inferior scholars for whom we have small redress, but especially by Mr. Booth (a Fellow of the College, and apparently of the Master's faction) their common instrument, who to our faces openly doth deride us, and some by name shamefully revileth, and offereth also further violence. The inferior scholars, whom the Statute otherwise ordereth, will not do us as much as common reverence; the Deans that have the government of the youth are resisted by them, and are so far from due correction that, being rescued one of another, the Deans themselves are shamefully abused, buffeted and beaten down, and the scholars therein maintained and encouraged." All this outrage is laid to the charge of the President—the "one Swayl" of Dr. Sandys' complaint—who "forthwith, by his absolute authority restored into commons and sizing (extra commons) the same scholar whom one of the Deans had before put out for his open contempt and intolerable abusage." This is dated July 18, 1582.

Further long depositions follow, directed against the same Mr. Swale, the President, and Mr. Booth whom he persisted in supporting. Thus, "Mr. Vavisour (another of the Yorkshire squires' sons), being a sober, wise young gentleman, said unto Mr. Church that he thought that his Tutor (Mr. Swale) was a Papist, because that when he requested him to buy him a Calvin's Catechism, or Beza's Confessions, he was offended with him and willed him to learn his belief and ten commandments, which were sufficient." "Item that Mr. Swale, being divers times complained unto, for that his pupils were corrupt in religion, made always this answer, that it made no matter for boys

what religion they were of, because they were
unstable and unconstant, and would daily
change their opinions." "Item that Cutting, a
singing man of the King's College, his ordinary
and almost only companion, being troubled in
mind, exclaimed against him, first in the open
streets and afterwards in his sickness, crying
out, Mr. Swale a dissembling Papist." "Item;
Mr. Swale, being complained unto of certain
scholars that were playing at cards in their
chambers, (a practice forbidden by statute
except during the general relaxation at Christmas), and that in the time of the sermon, he
used no reformation or punishment."

In the course of the dispute something more
is divulged about the suspicious Fingley, but
he is such a characteristic product of the time
that a fuller account of him is given further on.

The next charge, trifling as it may now
seem, was getting perilously near to one of
treason:—"Two young gentlemen of the house
made report to this deponent that they did
see a crucifix of silver and gilt about Mr.
Bapthorpe's neck (he will be mentioned later
on) as he lay in his bed." One of the clauses
of the Act of 1570 proclaimed that "if any
person shall . . . bring into the realm any
tokens, crosses, pictures, beads, or such like
vain superstitious things, from the Bishop or
See of Rome, and shall deliver the same to any
subject of the realm, . . . then that person so
doing, as well as every other person as shall
receive the same . . . shall incur the penalties
of the Statute of Premunire."

In the course of this deposition by Mr. Richard Gerrard we get a momentary glimpse of one of those deaths in College which were so sadly frequent under the insanitary conditions of the time: he "deposeth that Barnham was reported to be the bringer up of Huddleston deceased, which Huddleston had been instructed in papistry, and that the report was that Barnham did read popish prayers unto Huddleston in the time of his sickness; and that the said Barnham had written certain verses in commendation of the papists of our College. And further this deponent affirmeth that he did see wax candles carried to the said Huddleston's chamber by a serving man which he believeth were burning about the dead body until ten of the clock; and he affirmeth that he did see and handle red cloth which was carried to the said Huddleston's chamber to the end mentioned in the article, et aliter nescit deponere." John Huddleston, admitted in 1578, aged 17, was a son of Edmund Huddleston, Esq., and was born at South Weald, Essex. His family was well-known for its Romanist sympathies.

In the course of the dispute nearly everything that had been quarrelled over in the College, for some years past, is dragged into light: Mr. Gerrard concluded, for example, with such depositions as the following, which seem rather a descent from the high matters of Church and State with which he commenced:— "*deponit*: that the College is much annoyed with hackney horses: that the excessive lewd singing and organs; that it could not but be inconvenient; and he believeth that if *animalia* may not be nourished *ad delicias* that then such animalia are not to be maintained as do spend a great part of their time idly in music to the great trouble of others:"—and all this complaint before the piano had been invented!

So much must suffice for the goings on within the College walls. As regards the religious careers, and the vicissitudes or sufferings attendant on those who left the place with the resolve to stand by the old faith, one preliminary remark must be made. Those who fell under the penal legislation were either priests or laymen, the former being liable to capital punishment, the latter to heavy and continued fines. The best known of the priests were probably those who joined the order of Jesuits; but the seminary priests were much the most numerous. I give the names of all of both of these latter classes whom I have, so far, been able to determine. The evidence of their joining the Church of Rome, or becoming members of the Jesuit body in particular, is mostly drawn from Mr. Foley's "Records of the English Province of the S.J.":—but it was only in a few cases that he was aware of the Cambridge residence and training of the men whose names follow. The data furnished by our College records have therefore some historic importance.

The following members of our College are known to have actually joined the Jesuit Society.

The most famous of them was probably

Richard Holtby. He was a son of Lancelot Holtby, and was born about 1552 at Fryston in Yorkshire. The description of his father as being "mediocris fortunæ," does not of itself imply any very definite information as to his social status; but as he spent four years at Northallerton School the family must have been in fairly easy circumstances. He received part of his education at Caius College, having entered in 1573 after two years' residence in Christ's College. After a time he migrated to Hart Hall, Oxford, where he graduated B.A. in 1575-6. As a Jesuit priest his career was an exceptionally long and fortunate one; for though, like his brethren, hunted and dogged by spies and informers, he escaped apprehension, and after a long life of active wanderings, mostly in his native county of Yorkshire, he died peacefully in extreme old age, May 15, 1640. It is from the personal description of one of these informers that we gain the graphic touch that he was "a little man with a reddish beard." So remarkable does his immunity seem—he frequently visited York Castle, at the time that Henry Walpole was a prisoner there, previous to his execution—that Dr. Jessopp infers that he must have had some powerful friends in the background. He became Superior of the English Jesuits, after the execution of Garnet, May 3, 1606.

Another recruit was William Flack. He was the son of Walter Flack of Mellis, Suffolk, and entered our College in 1579 at the age of 18. His name was mentioned above as one of the little band that resolved "no longer to dissemble." He left the College soon after, and, with Gregory Seare, was admitted at Douay in February, 1582. He was ordained priest at Valladolid. He rose subsequently to be Rector of the Jesuit College of St. Omer, and afterwards of that of Ghent. He died in old age at St. Omer, December 13, 1637, aged 76. There seems no evidence of his having returned to brave the persecution in England.

Christopher Walpole was the sixth son of Christopher Walpole, Esq., of Docking and Anmere, a wealthy Norfolk squire of the same stock from which Horace Walpole was descended. He was a younger brother of Henry Walpole, of whose cruel torture in the Tower, and subsequent execution at York, a very graphic account will be found in Dr. Jessopp's work. He was admitted into the Society of Jesus at Rome, September 27, 1592. He was afterwards in Spain, and was confessor and spiritual father at the college of Valladolid; where he died in 1606. Like Flack he does not appear to have returned to run the risk of being hanged in England. He was admitted to our College in December 8, 1587, and was a scholar on the foundation until Michaelmas, 1590.

Robert Markham was a son of Thomas Markham, Esq., of Ollerton, Notts. He was admitted at Caius in 1584, but as he was not a scholar on the foundation, and did not graduate, there is no means of determining the length of his residence here. He appears at the English Jesuit College at Rome, August 1, 1593, and was admitted as a convictor, what apparently we should term a "fellow-commoner." He took the oath of admission soon afterwards. He left for Perugia in 1596, on account of ill-health, and died not very long afterwards at Loretto; without being re-admitted into the Society. From information supplied by Sir Clements Markham it appears that he was a promising youth, and had been for a short time in the employ of Lord Burleigh before joining the Romish Church. A letter from him to his brother Griffin (also a Romish convert from our college), dated from Rome in 1595, shows the difficult position of men of his religious views. He says that he had contemplated serving in the Turkish Wars, but could not obtain admission amongst the knights of Malta; and would not join any power at war with England.

Reginald Eaton was a son of John Eaton of Southwell, Notts. He entered in 1577, but we have no record of the length of his stay amongst us. He afterwards became a priest, being ordained at Rheims in 1587, joined the Jesuit order in 1610, and was fortunate enough to reach old age, as he died in 1641.

Charles Walgrave was of Cossey, Norfolk, and entered our College in 1598, a date when men of his sympathies were becoming scarce in the English Universities. He too belonged to an important family of Norfolk gentry: the present Earl of Waldegrave is descended from his uncle. After two years' study at

Cambridge, he went to Flanders. The Jesuit, Father Gerard, seems to have been the influencing agent in his change of conviction, as he was of so many others of the gentry of the Eastern Counties. Charles Walgrave entered the English College at Rome and joined the Jesuit Order. He received the Minor Orders at Rome; but as he was not a priest he seems to have escaped the capital charge, on his return to England. He lived for many years on his estate in Norfolk, as a lay recusant, doubtless suffering the heavy and continuous fines imposed on those of his opinions.

The list of "seminary priests," viz. of men trained and ordained at the various Roman Catholic colleges, who did not join the Jesuit Society, is a larger one. Some of these were regulars, some seculars: those at present identified as belonging to us are the following:

Robert Sayer (or Seare as he is called in our books) was a son of John Sayer, of Redgrave, Suffolk, and was admitted here in 1576 at the age of 16. His anti-Protestant opinions soon attracted attention in the College, and he was ultimately refused a degree with us; though he appears to have succeeded in graduating B.A. from Peterhouse in 1580. This was one of the grounds of dispute between the Master and tutors. Mr. Gerard, in his depositions, from which we have already quoted, complains that Dr. Legge "took displeasure against him for staying one Sayer from his degree, and upon that occasion made complaint of him to his father (Gerard's father was a prominent man,

Recorder and M.P. for Chester, etc.) at the Assizes in Lent, 1579." He afterwards became a Benedictine Monk at Monte Cassino, and gained celebrity as an author under the religious name of Gregory. In 1595 he went to the monastery of St. George, at Venice, where he died, and was buried October 30, 1632.

The connection of Richard Cornwallis with Cambridge life was longer and closer than that of any of the others. He was a son of Henry Cornwallis, Esq., of Coxford Abbey, Norfolk. He entered our College in 1585, and graduated B.A. in 1588, M.A. in 1592. He was one of the first Frankland fellows (December 21st, 1592), from which he passed to a senior fellowship which he retained until Michaelmas, 1596. He held more than one College office, being dean during the last year of his fellowship, and having been appointed "Humanity Lecturer" (what was afterwards called "Prœlector rhetoricus"), for the year commencing Michaelmas, 1592.

This last appointment is significant when we remember the proclivities of Dr. Legge, for the office was in the sole gift of the Master, and it was very rare, if not quite unprecedented, for it to be held by anyone not at the time an actual fellow. He was already thirty years of age when he entered the English College at Rome, being one of the many converts whom Father Gerard had gained over during his stay in Norfolk and Suffolk. He had considerable difficulty in making his escape from England, and suffered some months' imprisonment before

finally succeeding. He was ordained priest at
Rome 1599, and sent to England in 1601.
Luckily he escaped detection and lived to return
to Spain, where he died about October, 1606.

Edward Osburne was another student who
soon became notorious during his College
career. He was a son of John Osburne, of
Kelmarsh, Northants, and was admitted at our
College in 1574, at the age of 19. Like some
others, he was refused a degree at Cambridge.
He entered Douay, and was ordained priest
there in 1581, being soon after despatched to
England. Under the pressure of family
influence, and fear of State persecution, he gave
way and recanted, but seems afterwards to have
rejoined the Romish Church. In a letter from
the Recorder of London (Strype, Ann. III. 1-125)
he is thus referred to:—"One Osborne, a
seminary priest, came drooping into a chamber
where Mr. Topcliffe and myself were. Him we
examined, and it appeared that he was a seminary priest and had dwelt at the Hospital at
Rome four years, and after he was professed
into the house of the Franciscans, being bare-
foot friars that live by begging; and that he
lived by begging, and that he laboured by
cutting wood and bearing it on his back."

It was through him apparently that a fellow-
townsman was gained over to the same cause,
viz., John Roberts. This man was a son of
Lawrence Roberts, of Kelmarsh, and entered
our College in 1576. Osburne brought him to
Douay, after his first visit to England in 1583.
He went to Rome, where he was ordained priest

in 1587. He was got into England from Spain by a clever ruse of Father Parsons. He and a dozen others were sent over in the guise of English sailors who had formed part of the expedition against Spain, and had been taken prisoners. In spite of suspicions they escaped detection. He has been confounded with his namesake the martyr, who was, however, 14 years younger (v. Dom B. Camm's Life of Roberts).

Charles Yelverton, of Bawsey, was a son of Humfrey Yelverton, Esq., and was admitted here in 1590. Like Cornwallis, he was connected with the College for a considerable time, graduating B.A. in 1593, and (on the evidence of our register, though he does not appear in the University lists) as M.A. in 1597. He was a scholar on the foundation for seven years. He was admitted at the English College at Rome in 1601, through Gerard's influence. His own statement, on admission, contains an interesting account of his studies at Cambridge: "Sometimes I applied myself to the humanities; sometimes to philosophy; and, as it is the fashion everywhere, I was at one time eager to learn Greek, and at another Hebrew."

Henry Rookwood, son of Robert Rookwood, Esq., of Stanningfield, Suffolk, belongs to a well-known Romanist family; his brother Ambrose was executed for complicity in the Gunpowder Plot. He entered our College in 1579, but we have no evidence as to the length of his residence. In the MS. collections of both Davy and Blois, at the British Museum, he is described as a Romish priest; doubtless, therefore, he was a seminarist.

Another name may be added to the list of seminary priests with approximate certainty, viz., that of Nicholas Foxe, son of Thomas Foxe, gentleman, of Thorpe, Yorkshire. There can be little doubt that he was the Nicholas Foxe who was ordained priest at Douay in 1581. He had entered our College in 1573, but like most of those who seceded from the English Church, he took no degree here.

John Weldon, another seminarist, was executed at Mile End, October 5th, 1588. He is described as "some time of Caius College"; indicted "for that being born within her Majesty's dominions he was not only made priest at Paris by authority from the See of Rome," but had entered this land sent by the Pope. (Lansd. 982, p. 105.) He seems to have been a son of William Hewet, of York, captured in England (v. *The Month*, January, 1879).

William Deane, son of Thomas, of Grassington, or Linton, Yorks., was admitted a pensioner in 1577. His family connections seem to have been with the old faith, as his father is called a rebel. (Cath. Rec. Soc. v. 26.) He was ordained priest at Douay. Being sent to England he was soon captured, imprisoned, and banished. Returning, he was convicted on the usual grounds, and executed at Mile End, August 22nd, 1588.

Edward Dakyns, son of John, of Brandsburton, Yorks., was M.A. of Trinity Hall when he was introduced into the College. He

H

was tutor to R. Creswell, son of a Yorkshire squire, of a notorious recusant family, and was evidently one of the Master's supporters. The Fellows complain that "they did never hear of any punishment that the said Creswell sustained for his fault [absenting himself ostentatiously from chapel] and that his tutor was very unlikely to correct him for such a fault." Dakyns made the usual journey to Douay; was ordained abroad; returned to England and was banished. What finally became of him is not known.

The last name on my list is that of John Ballard. He, too, is well known, since he suffered death as a traitor, with the customary processes of being drawn, hanged and quartered, for complicity in Babington's plot. He is described as " Cantabrigiensis," and a graduate, at his first appearance at Douay, and as there seems to be no one else of his name—certainly no graduate—at Cambridge about this time, there can be no doubt of his identity. He entered our College in 1570, being a son of William Ballard, of Wratting, Suffolk. He was a seminary priest, but he cannot be fairly claimed as a martyr, since his death was distinctly due, rightly or wrongly, to political and not to religious causes.

One other name of decided literary interest may be added to the above list. It is possible that some reader may succeed in identifying the man beyond doubt. Henry Walpole, the eldest of the brothers and the instigating cause of the conversion of most of the other members

of his family, was present at the execution of
the Jesuit Campian at Smithfield. He was
deeply affected at the scene, and on his return
to his rooms in Gray's Inn he expressed his
feelings of grief and admiration in a series of
stanzas (printed in full by Dr. Jessopp). These
verses were sternly suppressed by the Government, and amongst the persons who suffered for
endeavouring to spread them was a certain
Stephen Valenger. He was condemned to the
pillory, and to lose his ears, and committed to
the Fleet prison in 1586, "for certain libels of
Edmund Campian"; these libels being apparently Henry Walpole's verses in commendation
of the martyr. He refused to divulge the
author's name. Now there was a Fellow of our
College of the same—very peculiar—name, in
Dr. Caius' time, who disappears from Cambridge
some years before the death of Campian. It is
highly probable that our Stephen Valenger is
the same man, but we should be glad of further
evidence.

The above list, with the exception of the last
man, is confined to priests or men in Romish
orders. In their case any return to their own
country involved a high probability of being
drawn, hanged and quartered. The names
which follow belong to a different category. It
comprises laymen, who were subject only to
fines. At least this was the punishment for
mere absence from the parish church, but, if
they went a step beyond, they incurred a good
chance of being hanged as well. For instance,
to harbour a Romish priest was a capital

offence. The father of one of our own students —Richard Langlaye, Esq., of Howthorpe, Yorkshire—was actually hanged at York, Dec. 1, 1586, for the crime of sheltering Romish priests in his house. This was two years after his son Christopher was admitted at Caius. The name by which these laymen were commonly known was Recusants, from their refusing the oath of allegiance in the form prescribed. They rendered themselves liable, by so doing, to a fine, simply crushing to all but the very wealthy, of £20 a month. The list of Recusants furnished by our College alone would probably be a long one; and the following names must form but a part of the list which could be compiled by careful study of the existent records in Fetter Lane, the British Museum, and the various Episcopal Registers.

For instance in one such list alone, about the year 1587 (Lansdowne MSS. No. 55), I find the following list of names amongst others:—

Norf. Mr. Jerningham of Cossey.
       Mr. Edward Rookwood and his wife.
       Mr. Thwaites that married Benningfield's daughter.
       Mr. Robert Constable, of Bowthorp.
Suff. Mr. Mannock, the elder, of Stoke.
       Mr. Mannock, the younger, with his wife and brethren.
       Mr. Benningfield of Redlingfield and his wife.
Ess.   Mr. Rooke Green, of Sampford.
Sur.   Mr. Nicholas Lusher, of Shoolands.
Salop. Mr. Bannister, of Wem.

Yks.   Mr. Ralph Bapthorpe, of Osgodby, and
        his wife.

Of these, Robert Jerningham was the father
of Henry and Thomas, who were admitted in
1589. Edward Rookwood is probably the man
admitted in 1575, brother of Henry the priest, and
of Ambrose of the Gunpowder Plot. Thwaites
is most likely Richard Thwaites, of Hardling-
ham, admitted in 1577. Robert Constable is
either our student of 1574 or his father. The
younger Mannock entered our College in 1564;
one of his sons became a Jesuit. Benningfield,
or Bedingfield, must be the father of our
student of 1608, as the latter seems to have
conformed, and was afterwards a Judge. Rooke
Green, of Sampford, had two sons here in 1564.
Nicholas Lusher is either our student of 1578
or his father. The same may be said of Mr.
Bannister, of Wem. Ralph Bapthorpe, of
Osgodby, was admitted in 1576. He died at
Louvain in 1617, and, after his death, his widow
entered a convent there, where she died six
years later. It deserves notice that of all the
men just mentioned only one seems to have
graduated; a tolerably plain evidence that an
English University at that time did not suit
the needs or requirements of this class of
gentry.

As was said, this list of Recusants concerns
one year only : it might be largely extended by
anyone who had the time to work through the
necessary documents. We should probably
find that besides the landed gentry above
included, and the avowed seminarists, there

was a considerable class of men who had studied sufficiently for the priesthood, but were debarred by scruple from English Orders, and shrank from the terrible risks attendant on those persons who were admitted to Orders by a Romish bishop. Almost the only career left to them was that of tutor or secretary in some wealthy Romanist family. Thus there can be no doubt that the Nicholas Goodrich, who was admitted in 1597 and graduated B.A. and M.A. respectively, in 1600 and 1604, is the same man who was returned as a Popish recusant in 1615, being at that time a private tutor in the family of Lady Sulyard, at Haughley, Suffolk. He had been a scholar on the foundation in our College. The following extract from the *State Papers* (January 1591-2) supplies another example: "One Kydman, a M^r of Arte, and student of late of Keyes Colledge, Cambridge, was there ; a noted papist; and is now one of my Lord's (*i.e.* Earl of Shrewsbury) secretaries." There were probably a number more of similar cases, but it is only by the most casual references that we can identify them.

One general remark may be made about the various men included in these notes. With very few exceptions they come from the country districts of England, and belong to the aristocratic, gentle, or at least superior yeoman classes. Of the crowds of youths who came to us from the large towns of Norfolk and Suffolk —from Norwich, Yarmouth, Lynn, Ipswich, Bury, and so on—I do not find one who swelled the ranks of the Romish priesthood, or suffered in pocket as a recusant. So far as this goes it certainly supports the common view that at the time in question, at any rate in the South and East of England, the dispute between Protestant and Romanist was much the same as that between the landed gentry and townsmen, between the agriculturist and the tradesman.

The facts thus roughly put together are but a fragment of what might be collected with sufficient time and labour. As originally compiled they were confined to the limits appropriate for a College Magazine; that is, they deal with none but members of our own College, and their nearest relations. But when we remember that the same influences were at work, more or less as the case may be, in every other College in each University, we can form some idea of the scale of what has been termed the "Counter-Reformation" of Queen Elizabeth's time, and of its importance in the history of the Church and of the nation.

VIII.

DR. CAIUS: AN APPRECIATION.

(Celebration of the Quater-centenary of the Birth Year of John Caius, October, 6, 1910.)

Our University and our various colleges have a long and noble list of benefactors to record. In not a few of these cases, if we enquire into the facts of their personal history, or read between the lines of the ancient deeds in our Treasury, we shall find that the wreck of an earthly life, or the utter disappointment of all family hopes, had something to do with the gifts. Our founders are not always, nor perhaps in the majority of cases, to be found amongst those whom the world commonly reckons as the prosperous and the happy.

But, amongst all our many benefactors, I doubt if, in some respects, a more tragic figure can be found than that of John Caius. Picture him, in middle life, about the time when he was contemplating the refounding of this college. He was already, by his industry and economy, in possession of an ample fortune, and might, like so many others in Elizabethan days—for instance, like his medical contemporaries, Wendy and Butts—have made it his ambition to "establish a family" in the country. That aim he entirely set aside. Or, he might have devoted his fortune to founding a new and important college. This he might easily have

done, and have left poor Gonville Hall to linger
on in obscurity and decay.   He preferred to
sink such personal ambition, and just to add his
name to the ancient and restored college.

At the age of 48 he handed over nearly all his
possessions to Gonville Hall, and then returned
to his hard work and lonely life in St.
Bartholomew's.   How lonely that life was we
know from a contemporary account.   Apparently he had, at that time, no other intention
than just to continue there till the end of his
days.   He practically gave his all, and then
went back to the drudgery of professional work.
I doubt if, in the whole long history of charitable endowments, we can find a case to set
against this:—one of such almost entire self-
effacement.

Two years afterwards, Thomas Bacon, whom
he had re-instated as Master in the enlarged
College, in such vastly improved circumstances,
died. The Fellows wisely seized the opportunity,
and begged their one help and hope to take his
place. He reluctantly consented. As he tells
us, he found the College on the verge of ruin,
through the negligence and inefficiency of those
in authority.   And this, notwithstanding what
he had already done for them.

As you know, his rule in College was not a
success. That is the pity of it, and what makes
his figure, as I have said, such a tragic one. It
could indeed hardly have been otherwise, for he
belonged, heart and soul, to an order of things
which was passing rapidly away ; or rather was
being roughly kicked aside.   In religion his

sympathies were with the ancient Faith. In
the University, what he cared for were the
teaching, the ceremonies, the discipline, even
the pronunciation, of the past.

In College he soon found himself confronted
by a turbulent band of Fellows: several of them
bitter Puritans: nearly all young—at the height
of the dispute the oldest of them was hardly 25
—hostile to authority, and supported in their
hostility by a powerful and growing party
outside. Not one of them achieved the slightest
distinction in after life, or seemed to feel
anything but angry contempt for what filled
the Master's heart with veneration.

It was a bitter and undignified squabble.
The Chancellor is appealed to. The University
authorities are invoked. The Archbishop is
dragged into the quarrel. The Fellows protest
that the Master is a tyrant: they denounce him
as a Papist: they also denounce him as an
Atheist. That was their side of the question.
The Master, on his side, was not voluble, but he
was certainly prompt and resolute. He proceeded to expel one Fellow after another. Nay,
if one of their pitiful petitions now in the
Record Office is to be credited, he set them in
the College stocks, and threatened them with
the rod.

Squabbles of this kind were unfortunately
only too common in our ancient Colleges,
though they were not often pushed to such
lengths. What is really unique here is the
serene and lofty spirit with which Caius, whilst
he continued to struggle with the individuals,

never ceased to study the welfare of the College.
Not for a moment did he falter in his pursuit of
the ideal which he had set before him.   No
insult or opposition seemed to have the
slightest effect on his designs.   He calmly
continued his benefactions.   He added fresh
estates to his already grand donation.   He built
a new court.   He gave many books, and valuable
plate.   He devised a new seal, and other em-
blems.   He wrote the *Annals*, and compiled a
set of Statutes.   One can really only compare
his attitude to that of some wise and devoted
attendant in a nursery of spiteful and fractious
children.   She slaps them and sets them in
the corner, as occasion requires, but nothing
that they say or do can make her for a moment
forget their best and highest interests.

But this could not last for very long.
Gradually Caius grew feebler, and more irritable
or more sensitive, whilst the opposition to him
spread and grew more virulent.   At last the
Fellows saw their chance and seized it.   They
got access to the Master's private rooms and
had a hunt there.   Keenly they must have
enjoyed the fun of rummaging about for the
" Popish trumpery " and the " Massing abomi-
nations " which they had so long denounced,
and which rumour said he kept in hiding for
the expected time of religious change.   They
found what they sought.   The next chapter in
the story is the strange and scandalous scene,
enacted in the court outside, when a rabble rout
of fanatics, headed by the Vice-Chancellor and
the Master of Trinity, might have been seen—

from 12 to 3, one December day—dancing round a bonfire like street-boys on a 5th of November. They were smashing and burning those symbols of the old faith which Caius had so fondly preserved.

Thus closed his career in Cambridge. He retired, broken down in heart and body, to his lonely home in St. Bartholomew's. And fools counted his life to be madness.

He paid one more visit, a very brief one, to his still beloved University and College. He was in the last extremity of weakness, and had to be carried on a litter. He just came to arrange matters for his successor, and to give directions for the construction of his tomb. A touching description is given of his weakness and suffering in his farewell letter to his old friend Matthew Parker.

I wish he could have been with us to-night; though I confess I should feel rather nervous about his judgment on my historical efforts. I seem to hear him repeating what he said to Parker: "Young men be so negligent now-a-days." Much, of course, of what we now say, and do, and think, would be utterly alien to him. But I would fain believe that he might notice some things of which he would fully approve. Consider these two:—The revived study and appreciation of the past, and the better understanding of ceremony and symbol.

When I first joined the College, the country was in the midst of what Carlyle, I think, called the "Scavenger age." Nowhere were the characteristics of the time more unfortunately displayed than in dealing with our old buildings and our old statutes. You know the fate of our ancient library. It was just gutted, and converted into sets of undergraduates' rooms, in which the occupant of a 15th century building might not be disturbed by the sight of anything which looked a day older than himself. That room, as you know, we have endeavoured suitably to restore. Perhaps some day the windows may be replaced: windows given by Bishop Lyndwood, the great canonist; by Boleyn, great grand uncle of the unfortunate Queen, and by other famous men of the past. Caius has described them.

Take, again, the ancient hall, still standing and in use till 1854. This room is, in a special way, connected with the memory of Caius. It was there that the ceremonial banquet was held, which he has so fully described in his *Annals*; when, in the presence of all the chief dignitaries of the University, he solemnly handed over his Charter of Re-foundation. That building has now been restored—like the library it had been defaced out of all recognition —and we may fairly regard it as being publicly opened to-day. The possibility of doing this we owe, as you mostly know, to the wisdom and generosity of our late friend and Fellow, Charles Monro. His memory comes back very vividly to me to-night, for it was at a table in that old hall that I first made his acquaintance, as we sat there on our arrival as Freshmen.

There is another point of sympathy; at least one in which the Spirit of the Age is tending

towards sympathy. If there was any one
characteristic which was dominant in the mind
of Caius it was the love of fitting ceremonial,
and the significance and help of symbolism.
There can be no mistake here. Every holiday-
tripper, as he is hurried through our courts, is
reminded, by the three well-known gates, how
it is through humility and virtue that the
young man should strive to attain to honour.
His Grant of Arms must, I should think, be
almost unique at the Heralds' College. Most
assuredly it is his voice, and not that of
" Norroy," that we hear, as the symbols are one
by one explained, and we are reminded that the
two serpents and their base indicate " Wisdom
with Grace founded and stayed upon Virtue's
stable stone." And in the solemn dedication in
the old hall, to which I have already referred,
the same notes are struck. He pointed to the
Cushion—it lies there on the table before us—
with the words, "We give thee the Cushion of
Reverence ":—to the *Caduceus*—there it is—and
said "We give thee the Rod of prudent Govern-
ance." And so on, throughout the ceremony.

But I must close. I have, I fear, employed
far too many words to be a suitable eulogist of
John Caius. You know his own sentiments, as
expressed by himself on the tomb in the chapel.
As Thomas Fuller said, " Few might have had a
longer; surely none ever had a shorter epitaph
—Fui Caius."

IX.

THE EARLY UNDERGRADUATE.

" *Studens Vulgaris*, or common British undergraduate. Variety : *Cantabrigiensis*. A hardy triennial. *Habitat* : abundant in meadows and by rivers, in winter and spring ; has been found also in chapels and lecture rooms. Flowers profusely in May and June. Seeds occasionally later on. Use in the Pharmacopœia: has been recommended as an irritant in obstinate cases of anchylosis, or tutor's stiff-jaw." (Old Herbal.)

It has been remarked, with some shrewdness, that if anyone wishes to know something about the life and habits of any particular class of men,—say the student of early times,—he will find some help in a careful study of the prohibitive legislation of the day. If it is desired to ascertain what he actually did, enquire what he was ordered *not* to do. If, for instance, he was peremptorily ordered to wear short hair[1] and a long gown, we may conjecture that, as a matter of fact, it was generally the hair that was long and the gown that was short. If he was forbidden to attend bull-baitings, to go fowling in Chesterton marshes, or to bathe in the river, we

---

[1] " That no scholler doe weare any long lockes of Hayre upon his heade, but that he be polled, notted, or rounded after the accustomed manner of the gravest Schollers of the Universitie, etc." (See Cooper's *Annals*, II 161, for the whole edict. With due insertion, or omission, of negatives it probably gives a good picture of the "scholler" as he occasionally displayed himself in 1560.)

gain a clue as to where we should be likely to
find him of a summer's afternoon. There is
much truth in this suggestion, for legislation is
not made at random, and it is seldom thought
worth while to forbid a practice until it has
become tolerably frequent. We shall therefore
find an appeal to statutes and college orders a
useful aid in studying the life and habits of our
friend.

The first fact to be impressed on the mind is
the extreme youth of the ordinary student, or
rather of the junior portion of the students.
This latter qualification is important, as it will
explain a good deal that is often misunderstood.
At the present day, the " man " is generally 18,
or more, when he enters; and he seldom stays for
much more than three years. In the sixteenth
and seventeenth centuries the "lad" was seldom
more than 16, and often under 15 or even 14, at
admission; and he very frequently resided for
six or seven years. The practical difference, in
respect of taste and habits between 18 and 22 is
slight; but the difference .between, say, 14 and
22, is enormous. Take, for instance, the practice
of flogging. The present-day student is shocked
at the bare idea of such a practice ever having
been tolerated. But I have never heard that the
sixth-form boy—say at the colleges of Eton and
Winchester—feels that *his* dignity is in the least
impaired when some one in the third or fourth
form suffers at the master's hands. So in the
olden days in the colleges of Cambridge. The
youth of 17 or 18 was generally as safe from
corporal punishment then as he is now ; in fact

decidedly safer than one of his age often was at
a public school a generation ago. Why should
the boy of 14 not be flogged at college as he had
been till the other day at his school? The
practice was common enough everywhere; and
his brother, in business as an apprentice, was
certainly not immune. And what else was to
be done with a rebellious boy of that age? You
could not "gate" him, for the entire college was
then, in the present sense of the term, perma-
nently gated. You could not curtail his cook's
bill, for he had none; and his ordinary allowance
of commons would, probably, bear but small
reduction. Impositions would be of small
deterrent force to one whose whole time was
already supposed to be claimed for work; and
as to fining him, the father would quickly be
heard from had that plan been attempted.
There was really no other effective resource, and
the only surprise to me is that the practice was
not much more prevalent than it actually
appears to have been. That it was occasionally
resorted to we know, though the popular legend
as to Milton's experience in this way is certainly
without foundation. But in our college I am
bound to say that I have never found a single
instance recorded or referred to. Fines, where
available; *i.e.* where the delinquent held an
office for which he was paid, or had reached an
age at which he was likely to have cash in his
pocket, are mentioned often enough in our
Gesta; and so are rustications and other penalties. But in all the various entries in our
college records, and in all the depositions and

complaints made in turbulent times, I have
never seen but one reference to the practice, and
that is hypothetical, or rather optative, as
describing what the tutor would have wished to
do. It was in the days of the Popish disputes in
Dr. Legge's time. The student was Thomas
Barwick, a gentleman's son from Westhorpe,
Suffolk. He was 16 at his admission, and must
have been a year or two older when he was sent
away for defiantly parading his "papistry";
declaring, amongst other things, that he would
not receive the sacrament because there was no
priest to consecrate. His tutor, Dr. Swale,
stated that he was averse to this expulsion, and
that, for his part, "he would only have beaten
him openly in the hall for the same, and so have
retained him, whosoever had said him nay, for
he was but a boy and so to be used."

The actual punishments recorded in our books
refer to such offences as would naturally occur
amongst a lot of young men and boys, living in
somewhat disorderly times, and many of them
with a rather rough bringing-up. The students
of that day do not seem, like schoolboys of
the past generation, to have indulged in pugi-
listic fights; or, if they did, no notice was taken
of this. But there are occasionally deeds of
violence recorded. Thus in 1627 John Gray, a
third-year student, was publicly admonished in
the chapel for assaulting an unfortunate sizar,
his junior by a year or two, and nearly knocking
his eye out: the offender is also ordered to pay
for the medical treatment of his victim. In
1608 Raphael Edwards, also a third-year student,

was fined ten shillings for attacking a freshman,
Jermy, "laying violent hands on him, pinching
him and turning him out of his bed-room";—
perhaps the fact that Jermy was a fellow-
commoner had something to do with the magni-
tude of the fine here. In 1627 George Drane, a
student of 21, was admonished because he had
struck another student with a stick, and drawn
a knife upon him. Somewhat later, in 1675,
John Dennis, afterwards famous as a dramatic
critic, was fined £3, deprived of his scholarship,
and recommended to leave the college, for
drawing his sword and wounding a fellow-
student; they were both bachelors of arts at the
time. This entry is interesting as showing that
the practice of wearing arms,—utterly at
variance with academic law and ancient custom,
—had begun to creep into college life.

From these accounts it would appear that
students, like modern sailors, carried their own
knives (presumably clasp-knives) for use at
meals, instead of having them supplied from the
kitchen. Dr. Caius forbids the wearing of any
arms "ultra cultellum ad ciborum usum." In
the inventory of Leonard Metcalf, a student at
St. John's, "a meat knife" is one of the few
articles of furniture mentioned. In one or two
cases, in our *Gesta*, assaults with knives are
recorded and punished, intimating that the
students had their weapons at hand. In fact
Caius expressly enacts (*Statutes*, § 50), that if
any student "abutatur cultello cibario, aut non
deponat jussus" he shall be expelled.

The same readiness of attack was not

confined amongst themselves, but was shown towards the Fellows also. Amongst the Gawdy MSS. (Brit. Mus.), there is a curious illustration of the manners of the University in the early Stuart period. The writer was young Gawdy's tutor. "Not long since your kinsman being at the College buttery at Beaver[1], at the permitted hour of the clock between 8 and 9 at night, the dean coming in charged him to be gone. He told him he would, and was presently departing. The dean told him, Unless you had forthwith gone I should have set you out. Upon that your kinsman, not brooking that speech, turns back and puts on his hat, and told him, Seeing that he used him so he would not yet out. Upon that the dean strikes him in the face with his fist. He, being a man of a spirit, could not forbear, but repays the dean with interest. For this he was convented before the Master and Fellows. He was deprived of his scholarship and warned within a month's space to provide for himself elsewhere." Gawdy was at this time a Bachelor of Arts.

The students' dress has always been a cause of trouble to their tutors, if not to themselves. The fullest discussion of their habits and tastes in this direction is contained in a report to Archbishop Laud in 1637:

---

[1] Beaver, or Bever as it is commonly spelt, was a slight repast, probably consisting of bread and beer, taken in the evening. It was not provided in the Hall, but those who wished went to the Buttery for it. Likely enough the occasion led to something of a social gathering there. It may be remarked that dinner was then about midday, and supper at five or six o'clock.

"The clericall habit appointed for students here is generally neglected unless it be in King's Colledge only, wherein they reteine the ancient manner both for color and fashion, with the use of square caps from the first entrance. At Trinitie, and otherwhiles at Caius, they keep their order for their wide Sleeve Gowns, and for their Caps too when they list to put any on, but for the rest of their garments they are as light and fond as others. And others, all that are undergraduates, wear the new fashioned gowns of any colour whatsoever, blew or green or ¹red or mixt, without any uniformity but in hanging sleeves. And their other garments are light and gay, some with bootes and spurs, others with stockings of diverse colours reversed one upon another, and round rustic caps they weare (if they were any caps at all) that they may be the sooner despised, though the fashion here of old time was altogether 'Pileus quadratus', as appears by reteining that custom and order still in King's Colledge, in Trinity, and at Caius, whose Governours heretofore were more observant of old orders than it seems others were. But in all places, among Graduates and Priests also, as well as the younger students, we have fair Roses upon the shoe, long frizzled haire upon the head, broad spred Bands upon the

---

¹ I cannot recall any other reference to this colour: Can it be a tradition of older academic usage? The Scotch student does, or did, wear a red gown " when he lists to put any on." It may be remarked that the present custom of each college having its distinct gown (blue at Trinity and Caius) dates only from the first half of the last century. Before then all the students alike wore a plain short black gown, as at Oxford.

shoulders and long large Merchant Ruffs about the neck, with fayre feminine cuffs at the wrist. Nay, and although ruffled shirts, 'Camiciæ circa collum rugatæ,' be expressly forbidden by the Statutes of the University, yet we use them without controule, some of our Drs, heads and all, to the laudable example of others" (v. Cooper, *Annals*, III. 280).

As regards their sports, naturally, those who had a chance were fond of frequenting the royal and aristocratic sport of bull and bear-baiting. But there were great difficulties here, for the University set its face against the pursuit within the limits of their jurisdiction, which for such purposes extended to four or five miles around the town. The attempt to secure the sport sometimes succeeded at Chesterton, though when the University Authorities got wind of the affair they quickly came down to check it. Thus, in 1581, Dr. Andrew Perne, Master of Peterhouse and Vice-Chancellor, writes to complain to Lord Burleigh, the Chancellor, of the way in which "the quietnes of our honest studies, in godly exercise of virtue, religion and lerning" is broken into. He encloses the depositions of the proctor, who reports that " upon a complaynt of the resorting to a bearebayting at Chesterton of a great multitude of younge schollers," the proctor, accompanied by the bedell and several Masters of Arts, proceeded thither. It was on a Sunday; April 22, 1581. " He there found the bear at stake, where he had been bayted in the sermon time, between one and two of the clock

in the afternoone. He asked the bearward by
what authoritie he bayted his beare there, who
answered that he was Lord Vaux's man and
had warrant from the justices." The proctor
replied that it was against the privileges of the
University, and "commanded this bearward to
cease from that disordered pastime, to which
the bearward submitted" (*Lansd.* MS. 33).
This was not, however, until the proctor and
the esquire bedell had had an awkward time of
it. The crowd "added contumelous speeches,
terming the proctour a petty officer, and the
vice-chancellour's man : whereat the standers
by began to showte and laughe at the proctour."
As to that dignified University official, the
bedell, he nearly took an active, but involuntary,
part in the pastime, for the crowd "violently
shoved and thrust the bedell upon the beare, in
sort that he cold hardly keepe himself from
hurt." It may be remarked that Chesterton
was always a favourite place for such sports;
and that the University often had occasion
to complain against the town how they
"endevored, by theire bearebaytinge and bull-
baytings, and such like vaine games, to hinder
the quiet of the Universitie, and to draw over
the students from their bookes."

Another, and safer place, for baiting the bull
and the bear was on the top of the Gogmagog
Hills. Till the middle of the eighteenth century
there was no enclosure[1] or plantation on the

---

[1] This enclosure has deprived us of what must have been
the most striking spot, for scenery near and far, in the neighbourhood of Cambridge. Every Cambridge man knows the

site of the Duke of Leeds' estate. The fine old
British camp of Vandlebury, now hidden by the
thick growth of trees, then stood out on the
bare downs, as such camps commonly do; and
the tracks, for there was no regular road,
straggled over the grass and through the camp.
This old camp was a very favourite place for the
sport, and though the wily proctor may have
lurked about the precincts of the town to inter-
cept his prey, on its way out or back, it is not
likely that he could effect much in such an open
country. By an order of the Vice-Chancellor,
May 29th, 1574, it is declared that "no scholler,
of what degree soever he be, shall resort or
go to any play or games either kept at Gog-
Magog Hills or elsewhere within five miles of
Cambridge."

The only game, in the modern acceptation
of the term, which we know to have been
largely played at this early date was football.
Historians of cricket like to trace back the
rudimentary forms of their science to an early
date; but its subsequent developments have so
altered its character that there is reason to

---

magnificent view over the fens still obtainable near there;
but from the camp itself crowning the summit of the down,
the view around must have been finer still. The spot, it may
be added, is one known to ancient legend. Readers of Scott
will recall the striking scene where Marmion rides into a
lonely moor at midnight, and blows his horn, to test the truth
of the legend that he would encounter a ghostly knight with
whom to break a lance. Many readers, however, do not
know that the original scene of the legend—placed by Scott
in the north of England—was this Vandlebury camp. (A full
account of the legend has been given by Mr. A. Gray, Master
of Jesus, in the *Proceedings of the Cambridge Antiquarian
Society*, No. LVIII.)

doubt whether we ought to use the same name to denote its earliest and latest[1] forms. But that a game which a modern spectator would entitle, as did those who played it in the reign of Elizabeth, "football," was popular, is tolerably certain. I have no doubt either that this is the game referred to in Caius' Statutes, under the term "pilæ reciprocatio." It has been fondly and vainly translated "catchball," but that Caius should definitely refer to it as a common practice, and prescribe that it should only be played in the College courts or gardens, and that no matches should ever be played with those outside the College, is proof of its popularity. And that such popularity cannot be ascribed to any other boys' game in Elizabethan times seems fairly certain.

Its early popularity is shown by a decree of the Vice-Chancellor, December 9th, 1580, which forbad any scholar " of what degree or condition soever he were, should at any place or at any time hereafter, play at the foot-ball but only within the precincts of their several colleges, not permitting any stranger or scholars of other colleges or houses to play with them or in their company, and in no place else. And if any person being not adultus shall break or violate any part of this decree and order, he shall for every default

---

[1] Since the game really became " Cricket " it has always been popular. The earliest local reference I have seen is in the Life of Henry Venn (student at Jesus, 1742-5). It is recorded of him that he was one of the best players in the University. Football, on the other hand, in spite of its early prevalence, seems to have died out absolutely for very many years, its present popularity being of recent origin (see the last article in this volume).

be openly corrected with the rod in the common schools by some of the University officers."

Anyhow "Fote bale" was freely indulged in, and matches with outsiders were carried on, all statutes to the contrary notwithstanding. The following report from the Vice-Chancellor to Lord Burleigh shows what sometimes came of these matches, and is an indication that Caius' restrictions were not so foolish as they might be thought. It is a complaint against the conduct of the parish constable of Chesterton, dated May 7th, 1581, about the same time as the bear-baiting incident.

"Thomas Parishe, being head constable, dwelling at Chesterton when ther was a match made betwixt certayn schollers of Cambridge and divers of Chesterton to play at the fote bale abowt two years past, the sayd schollers resorting thither peaceable withowte any weapons, the sayd townsmen of Chesterton had layd divers staves secretly in the church-porch of Chesterton and in playing did pike quarrells agenst the schollers, and did bringe owte their staves wherewith they did so beat the schollers, that divers had their heads broken, divers being otherwise greatly beaten, wear driven to runne through the river, divers did cry to Parish the constable to keep the Queenes peace, who then being a player at the foote bale with the rest, did turne to the schollers willing them to keep the Queene's peace, and turning himself to the townsmen of Chesterton willed them to beat the schollers downe." Another witness deposes to the same effect:

"When they were hotte in playe sodenlye one cryed Staves! and incontinently some came forth with the staves and so fell upon the schollers that they caused them to swymme over the water. And Longe John, servant to Mr. Brakyn, did folowe one Wylton, scholler of Clare, with a Javelyn; and if this deponent had not rescued him he beleeveth he would have run the said Wylton throughe." For his behaviour on this occasion the Vice-Chancellor succeeded in having the constable sent to the castle.

One recreation against which the University was especially severe was that of *bathing*. There is a decree of the Heads, May 8th, 1571, which is entitled, "That no one goe into the water." It is announced that if any scholar go into any stream, ditch, or other piece of water, whether for swimming or bathing, by day or by night, within the county of Cambridge, he shall on the first offence be sharply and severely scourged, openly and publicly, in his college hall, in presence of all the fellows, scholars, and pensioners; and on the following day again, with similar publicity, in the Schools, before his lecturer and his class, by the proctor or his delegate, shall be scourged, no excuse or petition to be listened to. On a second offence he shall be summarily expelled.

This unusually severe regulation has given rise to comment, and has been quoted as an illustration of the narrowmindedness of the authorities. It is quite possible that the prohibition is partly due to the natural impulse of those in authority, when they hear that

anything is being done, to send and tell the
perpetrator not to do it. There was, however,
somewhat more justification than is commonly
supposed. There was no[1] boating at the time,
and therefore if any student went into the
water it must have been for the purpose of
bathing. And in the general absence of neighbouring ponds it would naturally be to the river
towards Grantchester that they would resort.
But a glance at the Grantchester parish register
will show what a fatal place the river was then,
as it has ever since been. Over and over again,
both before and after this statute, is there an
entry of such and such a student—sometimes of
two or three together—being drowned within
the bounds of the parish. In fact, as is well
known, the repeated occurrence of such fatal
accidents in recent years has required special
regulations. I cannot but think, therefore, that
this recognised danger had something to do
with the prohibition, and was included amongst
the "many and grave causes" which called it
forth. It was the upper part of the river, above
Cambridge, which was then, as now, the
dangerous part, as it abounds with deep holes

---

[1] There may have been a little boating earlier; but, in
the absence of references, I should conclude that it did not
become common till the eighteenth century, and at first only
by the use of sailing boats. There was fine scope for this, as
the water communications in the neighbourhood were very
good, and access was thus easy to Whittlesea Mere, the large
lake near Ramsey long since drained. John Venn, of Sidney,
refers to such an excursion in 1782. It may be added that,
in a diary by the same, we have one of the earliest references
to boating on the upper part of the river: "October 23, 1779.
went in canoes up the Cam to Hauxton, with Gambier and
Wollaston."

and is much choked with weeds. It was here
that Byron's friend and contemporary, C. S.
Matthews, Fellow of Downing, an excellent
swimmer, was drowned. His screams and
struggles, when entangled in the weeds, were
remembered many years afterwards by some
who had been his contemporaries. The lower
part of the river was kept clear by the constant
barge navigation, and, being artificially widened,
was comparatively shallow.

The sporting undergraduate has always been
amongst us, and in early times his opportunities
in this way, so far as the authorities suffered
him to cultivate them, were unusually abundant
in the neighbourhood of Cambridge. Even as
late as toward the end of the eighteenth century,
Gunning tells us how, after lectures were over,
he had only to go as far as the marshy ground
—it commenced on the sight of the present
Lensfield Road—to make tolerably sure of
getting a shot at snipe. A few of the richer
students probably indulged in the high amusement of hawking—Dr. Caius expressly forbids
the keeping of "fierce birds." Some others went
in for hunting and coursing—in 1606 the
authorities issued an edict against those "who
have kept greyhounds and some of them
hunting horses, for coursing and hunting."
It must be remembered that in that day and
long afterwards—as we can see in Loggan's
maps of 1680—there was hardly anything but
open ground—"the fields" as they were called
—for many miles round Cambridge: and the
limitless marshes were close at hand.

Hunting and Hawking must of course always have been the amusements of the few, but the commoner sort had ample opportunities of indulging their taste. It does not cost much, as the modern schoolboy and those around him know, to start a catapult—and such, we may assume, was the nature of the weapon interdicted under the name of a "stone-bow"—; and armed with this he could follow his prey in the marshes towards Trumpington and Cherry Hinton. In 1606 the University after reciting how "divers scholars, specially of late years, have used to shoot in guns, crossbows, and stone-bows, where they have wandered abroad, to the destroying of the game and mispending of their time, ... they shall incur the penalties specified": *i.e.* if *non adulti*, of being corrected in the schools by the rod; and if *adulti*, of maken open confession of their fault in the said schools: in either case to lose a year for their degree.

Most of the faults for which punishments are recorded in our books are not of a very serious nature, being generally the pranks of high-spirited or mischievous boys. For instance, we find a couple of youths fined, and threatened with rustication, for "hollowing in the pump at night." Doubtless they had found a place where there was a fine reverberation; and we may conjecture that the authorities, after long and frequent disturbance in their slumbers, having at last succeeded in catching the offenders, were determined to make an example of them.

Perhaps the most characteristic distinction
in the goings on in ancient days, as compared
with modern, is to be found in the Christmas
festivities. Instead of the colleges being, as at
present, empty and silent at that season, they
were full of youthful and noisy life. Owing to
the difficulty and danger of long journeys in
the winter months, most of the students who
resided at a distance remained in College during
this season. There they kept high festival.
The hall would be at their service for masks
and revels, and for many kinds of games: a
good fire would be kept up in it for their
comfort: cards even were allowed;—this is
expressly mentioned by Dr. Caius in his
Statutes, as a concession for the season; and
doubtless many a song and story served to
enliven the long and dark evenings. There are
frequent references in our books and elsewhere
which indicate what scenes of mirth and
disorder the Christmas plays in the hall sometimes led to. For instance, in 1579, the Vice-
Chancellor complains to Lord Burleigh, the
Chancellor, about the conduct of one Punter, of
St. John's, "he was detectid of much disorder;
as namely that he had uncased, as they call it,
one of the stagekeepers of Caius College pluck-
ing off his visor"; that he had then proceeded
to make a disturbance at Trinity, and "had
almost set that house and St. John's together
by the eares." Finally, "to revenge himselfe
for that repulse had prively crept into Benet
College, and takinge upon him the habite of a
stagekeeper did assault one of Trinity, whom

also he afterwards challenged into the fields."
Such an entry also as this, from our Bursar's
book of 1616, is probably by no means a solitary
one, " for mending the hall windowes broken at
the comedie."

So much for the student himself and his
ways in College. But two other closely connected questions may be asked, as to which
there is so much prevalent misconception that
it seems convenient to offer a few words of
definite statistical answer. They refer to the
comparative social status of the student in
early times, and to the nature and locality of
the schools at which he had been trained. If
by "early times" we propose to go back 350
years, to the days of Queen Elizabeth (quite far
enough for present purposes), it may be asserted
with some confidence that there is one, and
only one, trustworthy source of information
on these points. That source is the Caius
College Admission Register, commencing in
1560. There is here recorded, by the wise
directions of Dr. Caius, full information as to
every student; in respect of age, birth-place,
parents' name and status, and, what is rarer
still, mention of the school, and often of the
Master's name, where he had been educated.
As far as is known, no other college in either
University has any records to compare with this
in respect of completeness and antiquity. The
Register has been published, so that the reader
can, if he pleases, verify or amplify the facts
adduced.

The complaint commonly urged takes some

such form as this: that the Universities from having been once the studying places of the poor, have become the idling places of the rich. Rich and poor are comparative terms, and need some explanation, and reference to time and place. Of course the average student of that day was very much poorer than his modern representative. But then, as a rule, so was his father, and probably to at least an equal extent. For instance. Sons of the country clergy have for 300 years formed a large constituent element amongst the students. Let any one examine and analyze a number of the wills of country parsons of Elizabethan times and he will soon realize how great has been the advance in respect of ease and comfort. A similar comparison would yield similar results in the case of the shopkeeper and the yeoman or farmer. If therefore class be compared with class there does not seem to be much difference between the past and the present.

What therefore must be intended, or should be intended, is that the proportions in which the students were drawn from the different classes in question have altered, and altered to the disadvantage of the poor as compared with the rich. Now this is a question which, whether important or not, must really be settled by appeal to facts. At the risk of seeming paradoxical, it is here claimed that no intensity of political convictions will by itself suffice to answer the question.

Let us start with 1564, by which time things were settling down after the religious changes

K

of the previous reigns, and take the first hundred entries in which details are furnished. The result is as follows:—12 of the parents are described as "Esquire"; 17 are "gentleman"; 8 are merchants or citizens of London; 4 are, respectively: nobleman, knight, doctor of medicine and doctor of divinity. The remaining 59 are described by a customary term "mediocris fortunæ." It need hardly be said that all the really poor must be found amongst these latter. But many deductions would have to be made. For one thing some of the families thus referred to are included in the Herald's Visitations, and were therefore *armigeri* or esquires. Again, there is abundant evidence to show that not a few were really well-to-do. For instance, Stephen Perse, the great Cambridge benefactor, belonged to a family which, judging by wills and similar evidence, ranked amongst the gentry. It is impossible to give convincing proof, but the general conclusion left on my mind is that, as regards class preponderance there is very little difference to be found between the past and the present.

Take another batch, 20 years later, viz. from 1584. The results are not dissimilar: viz. 26 Esquires; 23 "gentlemen"; 41 med. fortunæ; 12 yeomen; 9 clergymen (their sons are now beginning to become frequent); 6 London citizens; a sheriff; an LL.D.; and one described as "tenuis fortunæ."

Another way of regarding the subject is, instead of recording the social status described, to record the college status actually adopted.

We find 100 students thus grouped: Fellow commoners, 13; pensioners, 50; sizars, 37. This is a test of poverty, more than of social position. Sometimes the sizar was a younger brother of a pensioner; very frequently, especially in the following century, he was a clergyman's son.

The institution of sizars was the method adopted by our forefathers to enable poor men to obtain a College education. The sizar was boarded, lodged, and educated almost gratuitously, and he had in return to give his services. Some were called public sizars. These did the work of butler and steward; they are of very ancient standing, coeval with the origin of colleges. The majority, however, were of somewhat later standing. They were called "private," or "proper," sizars; and were assigned to the master, fellows, and fellow-commoners. They waited in Hall, and acted in every detail as valets to their employers. In all other respects they were treated as ordinary students. They underwent the usual examinations and exercises, graduated, obtained fellowships, and rose, according to their merits and capacity, to all the offices and dignities to which this was an entrance. Four out of the eight masters, who succeeded Dr. Caius, began their careers in this way.

The successive steps of the change at Caius College are fully recorded in my *Biog. History* (III. 274). Till 1703, the sizars who had waited sat down at the fellows' table, and finished what was left. In that year a separate table, with attendance, was provided for them: whether the remains were dished up and warmed, is not stated. In 1767 they seem to have struck against waiting at table; it was then agreed, "to allow the butler £20, and the remainder of the commons, to provide two servants to wait at the fellows' table." The change of feeling towards the sizar, and his consequent revolt, seem to have been the product of eighteenth century practice and sentiment. In 1745 the sizars were forbidden to wear the same gown as the pensioners. In so far then as special provision was made for the encouragement of poor students in old times this was the plan adopted. And if, what is by no means certain, a larger proportion of poor was then admitted, it was due to this cause.

All this is now a thing of the past; far removed from modern conventions. No one proposes to revive it. But when we pique ourselves upon the improved fellow - feeling to which the change is due, a few plain words seem called for. It need not be said that there is a lot of rough and menial work to be done, not only in a College but in the household of the most democratic of politicians, and in the rooms of the most reformed of clubs. The servants are doubtless treated with consideration and civility, but they are kept strictly apart, and no one will maintain that they are offered any prospect of advancement whatever except within their own department.

Our forefathers adopted an intermediate plan. A certain number of selected servants stood also in the position ·of students, and

enjoyed all the substantial advantages of
students. Their servitude was merely temporary. Not a few of them became Fellows and
tutors of the College, and in the course of some
years were in a position of authority:—very
possibly over the sons of their former masters.
Modern sentiment condemns this system.
It regards the whole body of the students as a
sort of family or society in a sense which cannot be predicated of a village, parish, or town;
and holds therefore that social distinctions
which are right enough in the latter must be
excluded from the former. Our forefathers held
that the distinction between the gentleman and
the small tradesman was an unquestionable
fact of life; why make a point of ignoring it in
College?

How this difference of feeling has arisen is
hard to say; but it is partly due, I suspect, to
the growing love of athletics, and to the greater
age and wider liberty of the students. These
causes tend to throw the members of one
college together into a more coherent body
than was formerly the case. In ancient days
there was very little of what we now understand when we talk of "College life." There
was no common boat or cricket club, no
musical or debating society, from which the
poor butler or steward would find himself
excluded by having to work in the kitchen or
buttery; or the "private sizar" from having to
attend to his master's wants.

When we try to look at the matter from
the point of view of our ancestors, another

consideration must be borne in mind. The position of "menial dependence" on the part of a youth, of the age of a student at that time, was not considered as at all degrading. Every one acquainted with the habits of the sixteenth and seventeenth century is aware that it was a common practice for poor relations to be employed in domestic service. And, to take a closer case in point, many of the younger sons of the gentry,—gentry in the strictest sense of the term, as being included in the Heralds' Visitations, — were apprenticed to city merchants. The duties demanded of a young apprentice were, to say the least, as menial as those demanded of a college sizar.

To sum up. The modern charge is that the sizar-system degraded a student to the position of a servant. The reply would have been that it raised a servant to the position of a student. Is it quite certain that the change marks the growth of real sympathy and appreciation between class and class?

Where did these boys get their schooling, and what sort of knowledge did they acquire? The question is one of some literary interest. Everyone knows what a dispute has raged about Shakespeare's opportunities in this way, and as to whether he really did pick up a little Latin and less Greek. Some, judging from the list of subjects directed to be taught at an important school, have gone near to assuming that he would have had the sort of chance which a boy would now enjoy, say, at Repton or Shrewsbury. Others have gone the length of denying contemptuously that a local school at a place like Stratford could have taught anything worth mention. Here again it may be well to consult the statistical facts available.

Had Shakespeare come to Cambridge he would have entered about 1579-80. I have selected 200 school-entries of nearly this date. They include the successive entries of pensioners and sizars; that is, the poorer class of students. Fellow-commoners are omitted, because they did not come really for the purpose of study; moreover they were often even younger than the others, and had been instructed by a chaplain or tutor at home. Owing to repetitions these 200 represent the schools of 107 students. The lads must have mostly come straight from school, as many of them were only 14 or 15 at the time of entry; and few were over 16 or 17.

The schools which head the list in respect of numbers are: Ely, Bury St. Edmund's, Norwich, Stevenage and Saffron Walden. The following list comprises all others from which three or more students are recorded: East Dereham, St. Paul's, Eaton Socon, Eton, Merchant Taylors, Aylsham, Stevenage, Clare, Harrow, Grey Friars' London, Ipswich, Holt (Norf.), Wisbech and Botesdale. Those, with one or two entries, are as follows: Aston, Ashby de la Zouch, Averham, Baldock, Barnard Castle, Bassingbourn, Bedford, Bennington, Belgrave, Boston, Boxford, Brandon, Brandsby, Braintree, Brentwood, Burton, Canterbury, Cambridge

(King's College School), Carlton (Yorks.), Chesterton (Cambs.), Christ's Hospital, Clithero, Debden, Denston, Diss, Elmdon, Eye (Suff.), Fulbourn (Cambs.), Gazeley, Giggleswick, Grantham, Godmanchester, Hardingham, Harborough, Heighington, Hickling, Hitchin, Holt, Kirby (Yorks.), Kelmarsh, Kettlethorpe, Laneham, Leeds, Leicester, Louth, Maldon, Marks Hall, Mattishall, Mercers (London), Monewdon, Newburgh, Northallerton, Nottingham, Rayleigh, Reepham, Rawcliffe, Rochester, Rotheram, Ryburgh, St. Bees, St. Antony (London), St. Neots, Saham Toney, Saffron Walden, Saxthorpe, Selworthy, Sheffield, Shephall, Shipdham, Snettisham, Southwell, Spalding, Stoke (Suff.), Thrybergh, Tibenham, Tideswell, Tonbridge, Tuxford, Twyford, Walsingham, Walkern, Warcop, Westminster, Weston, Worsbrough, Wymondham, York.

Such a list as this gives rise to some reflection, especially when it is compared with what a corresponding list of the present day would show. It is, of course, largely an East Anglian list, as is natural where Cambridge is concerned. Regarded as schools sending boys to College, many of the places mentioned will be strangely new to most readers. Of course it is not maintained that every one of them was a "school" in the strict sense of the word; it is possible that in some case it was a private venture of some local parish clergyman. But the fact remains that they were places where enough was taught to enable a boy to come up to the University. Wherever he was born he found such opportunities within a few miles of his house.

So far as the Shakespeare problem is concerned, the answer seems decisive. Unfortunately Stratford is not in the list, for very few of our students came from Warwickshire. But it is incredible that that county town should not have afforded the facilities obtainable in scores of smaller towns and villages.

Whatever the boys learned, or did not learn, at their school, it is quite certain that they must have acquired a fair knowledge of Latin. Most of them graduated and became parish priests. For their degree, and the preliminary exercises, that language was essential, and it was a common medium for use in the parish registers. Not a few became Fellows, and for all of these that language was one of daily use. They may not have been able to compose elegant verses in it, but they could mostly read and write it with ease.

As feeders of the University many of these schools have quite dropped out. Some have actually ceased to exist; others probably have not sent a boy to college for 50 years or more. To what causes is this due? I cannot but think that the main reason is the determination of the richer classes, quite irrespective of political opinions, to keep their sons apart, in schools by themselves. As there are not enough rich parents to support more than a comparatively small number of schools, the rest are starved. The determining causes of the selection may be various; the accidental presence of an unusually good master, a favourable position, or a better endowment. Some of the schools had a fixed sum of money left to them. As this fell in value all chance of getting good masters vanished; this was, for many years, the ruin of the Perse School, at Cambridge. In this relation two places in our list deserve a minute's notice; Fulbourn, Cambs., and Tuxford, Notts. From the information of the Vicar, I learn that the endowment of the former had become so insignificant that permission was obtained to divert the money to the Board or parish school. Tuxford still has a school building and a master; but, for the same reason, it cannot attempt anything but a merely commercial education. Enquiry would probably elicit similar explanations in other cases.

X.

ACADEMIC "SPORTS."

[Under this title were contributed from time to time short sketches of various eccentric members of the College. Such people hardly fall under the designation of "Academic Life"; but, as the reader will very likely not have made their acquaintance before, I have let them stand.]

The "sports" to be described here are not of the familiar sort which attract gate-money and lead to international rivalry. Any discussion of such as these would offer but small scope in the college history of centuries back. It is proposed to use the term rather in the botanical than in the conventional sense. We may take it for granted that the careers which a University training is mainly intended to encourage are of the sober, commonplace and useful kind. However much we may admire eccentricity, we do not expect that foundations shall be endowed for the purpose of propagating it. Genius will always take care of itself, but the main crop of the academic tree must be regarded as consisting of the successful and worthy clergyman, lawyer, doctor and so forth. And whatever else may be the merits or demerits of those whom we propose to record here, they certainly do not belong to any of these classes. It was not in the expectation of such fruit that the tree was planted.

Everyone who has been at school or college will have numbered amongst his acquaintance, and perhaps amongst his friends, men of the general type which follows:—Men of uncertain habits and probably of picturesque career; whose stay in college was always precarious, and whose departure was often abrupt; who, whilst they were amongst us were probably seen more than they were heard by their lecturer, and heard more than they were seen by their dean. They are a godsend to the College Biographical historian in his generally rather monotonous task.

1. A TURBULENT COUNTRY GENTLEMAN.

In the seventeenth year of Queen Elizabeth a young gentleman from Nottinghamshire entered our College. His admission is thus recorded in our Register: "Gervase Markham, of Laneham, Notts.; son of Ellis Markham, Esq. School, Laneham, four years. At St. John's College one year. Age 17. Admitted pensioner minor April 21, 1576. Tutor Mr. R. Swale. Assigned the first lower cubicle to the north, on the west side of the Caius Court." The first thing to be noticed about the young man is that he is *not* the distinguished bearer of that name. There was a famous author, Gervase Markham, also of Nottinghamshire, and probably a connection[1] of our man. He wrote a number of works on subjects which interest country gentlemen, and was, during the reigns

---

[1] Sir Clements Markham informs me that he was a fourth cousin.

of Elizabeth and James, one of the principal
authorities on the treatment of the horse and
dog, on the management of cattle and tillage of
the land, to say nothing of other subjects. Our
man, though he was the occasion of vigorous
correspondence on the part of others, did not,
so far as is known, ever pen a line of his own,
except in challenges to a duel and in one or two
letters to evade taxation.

He first became known to fame as one of the
principals in the desperate duel, "so much
talked of yet in these parts," as the author of
the notice in the old *Biographia Britannica*
remarks. The duel arose from a family quarrel
between Sir John Holles (father of the better
known Denzil) and the Earl of Shrewsbury;
the former having broken off a match with
the family of the latter in a way which was
violently resented. This was taken up by
Captain Orme, a retainer of Holles, who at once
fought with one Pudsey, gentleman of the horse
to the Earl. The result of this first affray was that
Pudsey was killed. Then Markham must have
his turn, and the historian tells us as follows:—

"Gervase Markham was a great confidant,
or, as the phrase is now, gallant, of the Countess
of Shrewsbury, and was usually in those days
called her champion. A proper handsome
gentleman he was, and of a great courage. He,
after Pudsey was slain, let fall some passionate
words, accusing Sir John Holles as the cause of
that quarrel, and as being guilty of his death.
This coming to the ears of Sir John he sends
him a cartel to this effect:—

For Gervase Markham.

Whereas you have said that I was guilty to that villany of Orme in the death of Pudsey, I affirm that you ly; and ly like a villaine, which I shall be ready to make good upon yourselfe, or upon any gentleman my equal living.

JOHN HOLLES.

Markham returned for answer that he accepted the challenge, and would accordingly give a meeting at such an hour alone, or, with either of them, a boy of fourteen or under; the place Worksop Park, and the weapons rapier and dagger. Sir John Holles, allowing of the other circumstances, excepted against the place being the place where his mortal enemy the Earl of Shrewsbury then lived, which he thought neither reasonable for himself to admit, nor honourable for his enemy to propound, and therefore urged that a more equal place might be assigned. Markham, taking advantage of this as if he had declined the encounter, published it accordingly to his disgrace. Holles finding this unworthy dealing, and that he could not have an equal place assigned him, resolved to take that opportunity which fortune should next offer him, and such an one shortly after offered itself. To the Christening of his second son Denzil, the Lady Stanhope his mother-in-law was invited as god-mother; after which performed she returned from Haughton to Shelford. Holles, accompanying her part of the way over the forest of Sherwood, it fortuned that Markham with

others of his company met them and passed
by. So soon as he saw that Markham was
passed, he took leave of Lady Stanhope, galloped
after and overtook him. When, observing how
unworthily he had dealt with him, they both
alighted and drew their rapiers. I have heard
him say (the writer was a cousin of Markham's)
that upon the first encounter he used these
words, *Markham, guard yourself better, or I
shall spoil you presently;*—for he said he lay
as open to him as a child : and the next pass
he ran him through (the lower part of his
body)—up to the hilt, and out behind towards
the small of the back. With this wound
Markham fell, and was carried off the field by
those in his company, whilst Holles, with his
servant and a groom who only were with him,
returned to Haughton. The news coming to
the Earl of Shrewsbury he immediately raised
his servants and tenants to the number of
a hundred and twenty, with a resolution to
apprehend Holles, so soon as he knew that
Markham's wound was mortal; which Lord
Sheffield, afterwards Earl of Mulgrave, understanding, he speedily repaired to Haughton,
with three score in his retinue out of Lincoln-
shire, to assist his cousin-german, in case the
Earl should attempt anything. An old servant
of Holles told me he was present when Lord
Sheffield came, and that his master going forth
to meet him, he asked him how it was with
Markham, he replied that he thought the
greatest danger was that he had spoilt his ——
(misbehaviour). I hear, cousin, says Lord

Sheffield, that my Lord Shrewsbury is prepared to trouble you; take my word, before he carry you, it shall cost many a broken pate. And he went in and remained at Haughton until they had certain account that Markham was past danger, who indeed recovered and lived after to be an old man, but never after eat supper nor received the sacrament; which two things he rashly vowed not to do until he were revenged.

Thus much of his history Carlyle was acquainted with, and in his *Essays* (IV. p. 316) has given, from the same source, some account of the duel. But he does not seem to have known, though it would have much interested him, certain later experiences of this disreputable old gentleman. During his middle life Markham seems to have been in the army, and, on the authority of his tombstone, to have performed good services in Ireland and abroad.

He finally appears, in the clear light of history, during the troublous times preceding the Civil War, when the "*State Papers, Domestic*" have a good deal to say about him. The Sheriff of the county writes (January 26, 1635-6) that Markham will not pay his tax: "at the time of the assessment he found not any one refractory except Mr. Markham . . . . Out of £800 per annum in land, and as it is thought £40,000 in money, he spends not £40 in all manner of expenses, and has none to leave all this to but two bastards that he will not acknowledge."

This was in consequence of Markham's reply
to the Sheriff's demand "If he had been commanded to present to him his head, he would
as willingly have done it." A few days later
he complains that Markham "had reproached
the Sheriff with ill language." On this the
Lords of the Council ordered him "to render
satisfaction to the Sheriff, and to be conformable, or to expect to be called to a strict account."
Next appears the sergeant-at-arms, who had a
warrant from the constable to arrest the
delinquent. But it does not seem that much
came of this. It is reported (March 4, 1635-6)
that "Markham is so infirm and useless in all
the parts and members of his body that he is
not portable to London. He has not been able
to stir out of his chamber these five years, nor
has he been able to come out of his bed these
two years." Apparently however the apparition
of the sergeant was at last effectual, as a letter
is sent by Markham himself (March 12) imploring
the king's pardon "in the humblest manner
that his heart can devise," and dated "from
his poor house at Dunham." It is plain from
the terms of his letter that his refusal to pay
the tax was due to no feelings of patriotism,
but was the obstinate resolve of an old miser.
His end was not far off; and the next, and
last, that we hear of him, is the assurance of
his monument, a stately erection in Laneham
Church, that "he was captain of the Horse in
the said county (Notts), who long served her
Majesty in her war, with extraordinary proof,
in Ireland, and the Low Countries."

L

2. A Seminarist Martyr.

In a previous essay *(An Elizabethan Episode)* there are references to a supposed Popish priest, or spy, said to have been introduced and encouraged by the Master, and who was called Fingley. As no such name was to be found in our Admission List, there seemed at first some reason for supposing either the name was an *alias*, or that the imagination of the Protestant opponents of the Master had been allowed too free play. Such suspicions have been since found to be unjustified. John Fingley was a real person, and one of those—not few in number—who sealed their faith by martyrdom. He was a Yorkshireman, like the Master, Dr. Legge, and the President, Mr. Swale, and was born at Barnby. Of his family nothing seems to be known; but, as he entered as a sizar, he probably sprang from a yeoman or trading stock, rather than from amongst the gentry who at that time formed the great bulk of the sympathisers with the Romish Church. He matriculated as a sizar, from Caius College, December, 1573; but, as already stated, his name does not appear in our Admission Register. This may have been an accidental omission, but in the light of subsequent disputes it looks more as if the registrar of the college had deliberately excluded him. He first appears as the sizar, or domestic servant, of Hugh Crescy, son of Nicholas Crescy, Esq., of Blyth, Notts., a pupil of the Master. He was soon, however, taken up by Dr. Legge, who put him into the place of college butler. This was a very ancient office, dating indeed from the time of the original statutes of Bishop Bateman, and one which was always held by a student of the college. The butler and steward were what were called *public* Sizars, as distinguished from the private or *proper* Sizars who waited on the Master or individual Fellows. They had strictly defined duties in respect of looking after the amount and quality of the food supplied in college, and always ranked amongst the scholars. In fact they were termed pre-eminently "foundation scholars," or "scholars of the college," in order to distinguish them from those now understood by the name, and whose endowments were the results of private beneficence. As college officers they were appointed by the corporate body, and this was the ground of much of the complaint about the man in question, as the Fellows objected that Fingley had been unlawfully intruded by the Master's sole authority.

As regards his college career, our source of information consists of a quantity of depositions and complaints now preserved at the British Museum (MS. *Lansd.* 33). They are the outcome of one of those quarrels between Master and Fellows which seem to have been almost the normal state of things in former days. In this case the majority of the Fellows were much incensed against the Romish proclivities of the Master, who, they asserted, took every opportunity of encouraging Papistry. As to Fingley, they made up their minds that he was

a priest in disguise, and that he had been
introduced into the college for the sake of
performing private mass at the lodge, or the
rooms of other secret Papists. In this complaint they were apparently anticipating, for
he was probably not ordained till later, but
there can be no doubt that they were right in
their judgment of his sympathies and efforts.
The following are the principal passages in
their depositions—addressed to the Chancellor
of the University—which refer to Fingley:—
"Item. That one Fingley, belonging to the
Master, and made butler of the house by him
without consent of the Fellows, was a great
perverter of youth in the house, and one that
never came to prayers nor sermons, as the
Master well knows, and yet greatly favoured by
him." . . . "That Barwick (one of the
President's pupils) made answer that he had
heard there was a mass said by Fingley in our
Master's great chamber over the parlour."
. . . "That Sayre (a student who afterwards
became a Benedictine monk) had been of great
familiarity with Fingley, a pernicious Papist."
. . . "That Fingley did first attend upon Mr.
Cressy, the Master's pupil, and afterwards upon
the Master himself (*i.e.* as sizar), and that he
was made butler of the house by the Master
without consent of the Fellows, and contrary to
the statutes of the college, which is a proof that
the Master greatly favoured him, and that the
common rumour was that the said Fingley did
labour much to pervert youth secretly; and he
well knoweth that the same Fingley came very

seldom or never to prayers or sermons, neither
did he ever hear the said Fingley was sent away
by the Master on any displeasure, but that his
lewd dealing being detected he ran away for
fear of further punishment by others."

From all this it seems clear that Fingley was
already an earnest and active supporter of the
Romish cause. He came to the college just at
the most critical time. The majority of the
Fellows were certainly on the Protestant side,
but the heavy weight of the Master and
President was in the other scale, or at least
was supposed to be so; and this supposition
was quite enough to bring to the college a
crowd of young gentlemen—largely from the
Master's own county, Yorkshire—many of
whom were avowed Romanists, and many more
in decided sympathy with the old faith.

Of Fingley's subsequent career there is not
much to say. It was very short, and ended, like
that of two or three of his college contemporaries, on the gallows. He appears to have
resided within our walls for about three years:
and then, for a short time, disappears from sight.
He was admitted at Douay College, the principal
training place for the seminary priests, February
13th, 1579-80; where the *Diary* says of him.
" venerunt ex Anglia duo juvenes, Christopherus
Ingram et Joh. Fingley, Cantabrigienses, qui
statim se Theologiæ studio addixerunt, et ad
communia nostra admissi sunt." He was
ordained sub-deacon, February 21st, 1580-1; and
priest by the Bishop of Chalons, at Rheims—
where the college was temporarily situated—

March 25th, 1581. He was sent to England,
April 24th, 1581, just about the time when his
name was being so much mentioned in the
depositions above referred to. He does not
appear to have revisited Cambridge: his name
could hardly but have been referred to if he had
—but probably went at once to his native
county, Yorkshire, and worked there during the
few years which were left to him. We catch
one glimpse of him in prison, when he is
referred to as "priest of God, put into a low
prison, into a deep and darksome dungeon," at
York. Nearly all else that is known of him
may be given in the words of Bishop Challoner,
the historian of the sufferers belonging to the
Romish faith. "After many labours in gaining
souls to Christ in the northern parts of
England, he was apprehended and committed
to York gaol; and being brought up to trial was
condemned for high treason, for being a priest
made by Romish authority, and for having
reconciled some of the Queen's subjects to the
Church of Rome. He was hanged, bowelled,
and quartered at York, August 8th, 1586; and
suffered death with a generous courage."

3. An Astrological Fellow.

Towards the middle of Queen Elizabeth's
reign a young man from Yorkshire entered our
College. His origin and training are thus
described:—"John Fletcher; son of Thomas,
husbandman. Born at Hebden, Yorkshire.

School, Leeds, under Mr. Hargraves, three years.
Age 21. Admitted pensioner, February 5, 1577-8.
Assigned a cubicle, with his surety Mr. Paul
Gould, M.A., fellow." He was a scholar on the
foundation. Graduated B.A., 1580-1; and M.A.,
1584. Became a Fellow of the college about Lady
Day 1587, and remained so till his death, October
14, 1613. He held the college offices of catechist,
bursar, and salarist; and was for some years a
tutor in the college. He was buried in the
college chapel, where there was formerly a
monument to his memory.

Such are the mere facts of his academical
career; but he seems to have acquired a wide
reputation, in England, in a department of
Applied Mathematics never much encouraged in
the University, and now discredited under the
name of *Astrology*. He was, for instance, constantly consulted by Sir Christopher Heydon
during the writing of his *Defence of Judicial
Astrology*. We have now, in our library (MS.
No. 73) nineteen letters to him from Sir Christopher, full of questions upon obscure points in
his science:—these letters were doubtless placed
there after Fletcher's death. The father, it may
be remarked, had chosen Fletcher as his son's
tutor, presumably on account of his special
reputation. Most of these letters are occupied
with technical points of no present interest, but
there is an incidental remark in one of them
which deserves notice. Sir Christopher asks
Mr. Fletcher to *cast his son's nativity*. This is
a duty which seems to have dropped out of the
modern round of college demands on the part of

parents and guardians; though I have not the slightest doubt that our present indefatigable tutors would rise to the occasion at once, if the demand were made upon them, and cast the nativity of any pupil who would supply them with the requisite data. If they want to do this, it may be remarked they have now the advantage of being able to employ Fletcher's own astrolabe for the purpose. Fletcher's reply as to young William Heydon's future career is unfortunately not to hand, as none of his letters are preserved. This is a pity, for the young man's career was a tragic and peculiar one, and would have given a good opening to the tutor for an exact forecast of his pupil's fate. He fell in the ill-managed expedition to the Isle of Rhé under the Duke of Buckingham in 1627, where "he was carried by a rabble of flying soldiers into the sea, and there drowned."

At one time Fletcher came into a certain public notoriety, and a good deal is to be found about him in the *State Papers, Domestic.* In January, 1592-3, a certain Mrs. Jane Shelley, of London, got into trouble, or at least into suspicion about matters religious and political. It was an awkward position at any time in the reign of Queen Elizabeth, and especially so just after the time of the Armada. The exact grounds of suspicion against her do not appear, but we gather that one person at least whom she consulted feared that "there would be alteration and rebellion before long." Her own contention was that she had only wanted to know about her private affairs. She admitted

that she "had a conference with Fletcher, of
Caius College, said to be skilful in Astronomy,
and moved him to set a figure how she should
recover certain money and jewels; he told her
that she could hardly get them, as Baxter (the
delinquent) had pawned them." (We are not
told whether this was a scientific deduction on
Fletcher's part, from Astronomical data, or
whether Mrs. Shelley had unintentionally let
out the fact.) Then she enquired about her
husband, "he being a prisoner and a dead man
in law, and whether he would escape that year
or the next, but he made her no answer." Then
she asked about her deed of jointure, which some
one was keeping from her, but according to her
account Fletcher here became still more oracular,
for he only replied that "knaves be knaves."

The above is the lady's account, from which
one would almost gather that she had just run
down by the morning train for a consultation
with the occult authority. Really she seems to
have paid a visit of some duration, and to have
extracted a good deal of amusement out of it,
considering her husband's very awkward position
at the time.

Now follows Fletcher's own defence, as given
in his deposition before the Privy Council in
London. I give a full copy of the original in the
Record Office; the summary in the printed
Calendar is not merely (as it should be) very
brief, but by a blunder nearly all the most
graphic part, referring to our College Courts, is
attributed to some one having no connection
with us. He says:

" February 17, 1592-3. Mrs. Shelley cam to my chanber about Midsomer was a twelve-month, and demanded of me how she might recover certaine things againe from a minister, Nathaniel Baxter, who had deceyved her of them: to whom I answered, to sue him in Lawe would tend to her great infamy, besides the charges. Then she said she had a good friend Mr. Pechover in London, to whom I counsalyed her to repair for his helpe. In my window laye some Goozeberyes latelie gathered, which she tooke and did eate. Thereupon, to pleasure her, I said that there were more in the garden[1]; whether she was willinge to goe. Wherafter she had gotten a few more goozeberies we walked four or fyve times in the alley. When I demanded of her whether she was widowe or wife; she said, I have a husband, yet as though I had none, seinge he is a dead man in lawe; and thereupon told me what had befallen her husband. Asked me yf I could tell whether her husband should escape deathe in Januarye or Februarye followinge, whereof she doubted. I answered that I was lothe to deale in such matters, and yet I could do her noe good except

---

[1] Presumably the same as the existent garden in the Tree Court. It was, of course, larger in those days, as, until the erection of our present New buildings, it extended as far as Trinity Lane. Being surrounded by a high wall it was well secluded. Very likely much of the rest of the Tree Court may have served the same purpose. This was mostly bought by Dr. Caius in 1565; but until the erection of the Legge and Perse buildings, some sixty years afterwards, was perhaps also used as a college garden. The hinges of the gates which closed it are still remaining inside the archway of the Gate of Virtue.

I had her husband's nativitie; thinking thereby
to shake off her question; so after that tyme
she departed. An other tyme she cam to my
chamber, but she would not staie, because she
said Mr. Butler[1] the physician had greatlie
rebuked her for cominge to schollers' chambers.
So I walked with her abroad into the fields,
where she was importunate with me to resolve
her the question of her husband's deathe. But
I answered her that I could not pleasure her.
Amongst other talke which I have forgotten
she asked me if I had heard of a night spell. I
said noe; for I never regarded such matters.

"An other tyme upon a Sondaie in the
afternoon, after sermon, she sent her laundresse
to me to desire me to come to her in Mr.
Bradshawe's garden, to whom I answered that
I was lothe to be seene with her so often alone,
especiallie seinge I could do her no good; and
bade her tell her Mrs. that now I could not well
come, but an other tyme I would come to
her. But Mrs. Shelley shortlie after sent one
Tompson the clerke of St. Edward's parishe,
whom by chaunce she met in the street, to me
againe to desire me to come to her in the
foreseyd garden.[2] Then to satisfie her, I went
to her in the said garden; where she sittinge

---

1 The well-known Cambridge doctor: "the most celebrated physician of his age" (Cooper, *Annals*, III. 119). He
was a fellow and benefactor of Clare College.

2 The reference to the 'alley,' and to the likelihood of
other Fellows coming in, make it plain that this garden is, as
before, part of our Tree Court. I do not know what 'Mr.
Bradshaw's garden' was: possibly an adjacent plot, or one
now included in the 'president's garden.'

and I walking up and down by her in a streit
alley where twoe could not walke together, and
said: 'You will not sitt because I smell of
garlick, which I have eaten to amend my
stomacke.' To whom I said, 'I doe not like your
physick, neither do I refuse to sit down therefore, but because the seat would beraye my
gowne; as also some of the house who might
come into the gardeyn should not see us sitt
together.' Then after she tould me divers
histories of persons and famylyes, who were
decaied and overthrown (whose names I do not
remember, not greatlie attendinge her speeche);
but, said she, if troubles should arise those
persons who heretofore had hardlie dealt with
others might possiblie be hardlie dealt withall
againe. To whome I said, as I remember, that
it was not for her or me to deale in these
matters, but praie to God that such troubles
might not ensue; and those persons who now
did most desire then might soonest feele smarte
therefore. Amongst other speeches at lengthe
she said: And in faithe what saye you of my
husband. Whether shall he escape or noe? To
whom I said: Mrs, I can doe you noe good in
these cases. And nowe I must leave you,
because I must go to praiers nowe att fower
oclocke. And so I departed.

"An other tyme she came into our colledge
courte, and there walked a while; and meetinge
with a scholar of our colledge called Codlinge
she sent him up to me to desire me to come to
her in the court. When I came we walked a
turne or twoe and then she rested in the porche

of the colledge called *Porta Honoris*, and took furthe a booke, whether printed or written I knowe not, and said, I have been readinge of this. At length she said: Seinge you will tell me nothinge, tell me what husband my mayde (whom I love) shall have; to whom I said, Yf you will be so good as bestowe some porcion on her to helpe her to a good husband, doubtless she shall doe well. I see, saieth she, you are not willinge to tell me anythinge, and so I leave you. And so departed discontented, since which tyme I never see her nor heare of her."

One would willingly have another glimpse of Mrs. Shelley; but unfortunately, History itself, like Mr. Fletcher, can only say that it "never see her nor heare of her" again. But it is a queer picture we get of this garralous dame fluttering down from London to our quiet college courts to consult the astrologer about her own property, and her maid's prospects in life, and whether her husband was to leave her finally next January, by way of Tyburn. As she flirted, on a midsummer day, amongst the gooseberry bushes in the Tree Court, or on the secluded bench in the Gate of Honour (then generally kept shut), did it cross her mind that Fellows of colleges might marry,—some time after January, or when they had obtained a living? If so, she was disappointed, for Fletcher stuck to College, and died there twenty-three years afterwards.

As I have said, Fletcher's own *Astrolabe* is now in our Library, available for the use of his successors in the tutoriate. An expert in such matters (Mr. Knobel), who has kindly examined it, has dated it about A.D. 1490; so it was already of some antiquity when it came into Fletcher's hands. It is referred to in the College *Annals*, where Fletcher is said to have given us a *sphaera aenea cum capsula*. The case is, I understand, a feature of considerable interest about the instrument, being a very fine specimen of stamped French leather work.

4. A BISHOP'S BLACK SHEEP.

Soon after the Restoration a youth entered our college, whom Titus Oates must have looked up to as a senior, and from whom even he might perhaps have learnt something. His admission entry runs thus:—Francis, son of John Buxton, gent., of Edgefield, Norfolk. Born at Saxthorp. Schools, Holt and Norwich. Age 16. Admitted sizar, June 27, 1661, under Mr. Ellis.

His career was an utterly shabby and disreputable one, but it helps to illustrate the times: and it certainly shows one of the difficulties under which ecclesiastical discipline had to be carried on in England. The racy and outspoken language of the Bishop, Dr. Lloyd, is perhaps the principal redeeming feature in the story.

Mr. Buxton began badly whilst a student, for it is recorded of him in our *Gesta* (April 20, 1664), that he was "admonished the second time for a fault too gross and heinous to be recorded." Presumably the supply of clergy was short at this time, just after the Restoration, and the authorities did not see their way to being too particular. Anyhow this incident did not stop his career; for he graduated B.A. and M.A. in due course, and retained his scholarship till 1668.

We next hear of him as being ordained at Norwich (not by Bishop Lloyd): deacon, Jan., 1673, and priest the following March, to the curacy of Runcton, Norfolk. What scandals he may have created there we have now no means of knowing, unless the parish register may throw any light on his misdoings. But a few years later we hear enough of his behaviour from the graphic pen of his diocesan. Amongst the MSS. known as the Tanner Collection, now in the Bodleian Library, are a number of letters from Dr. Lloyd, then Bishop of Norwich, from which the following extracts are taken.

Writing to the Archbishop of Canterbury, February 22, 1685-6, he says: "There is an untoward clergyman now in the gaol here whose name is Buxton. He is guilty of horrid villanies. He was suspended by Bishop Reynolds, excommunicated by Bishop Sparrow, and since my coming he hath . . . . He shot a brace of pistols at a shopkeeper in this city, charged with bullets; and the last week he quarrelled with a poor housekeeper here and smote him with a weapon called the Protestant Flail, and the poor man is desperately wounded. Upon this he was committed, and I told the justices not to bail him." The Bishop then goes on to enquire whether a cleric may be degraded in any case which is not capital. The next letter about him is a few months later, viz. June 4, 1686. "I had him safe in prison in the castle of this city (Norwich). But the King's gracious pardon set him at liberty: and thereby insured him, as it did many more, from any further proceeding from me." Buxton at this time was promising amendment, and was desirous of obtaining a licence to preach. Apparently he obtained it, after making public confession and recantation of his offences of drunkenness, profanity and incontinency. Once more the Bishop writes, April 1, 1687, as follows: "My old friend Buxton whose submission and confession your Grace hath seen, hath, in the Passion Week, adventured upon a clandestine marriage. The motive was five guineas, as I am informed. The young woman's name was Mrs. Rant, an orphan, her portion £1500. I do not know what to do with the villain, for he hath neither benefice nor cure; and therefore no suspension but that of civil magistrate can reach him, viz. that sovereign one *per collum*."

What became of Buxton after this we do not know. Perhaps he drifted up to London to enlarge his business of carrying on clandestine marriages. Those who think that the characteristics of the "Fleet Parsons," as pictured by Fielding, Smollett and others, are exaggerated, will understand that, with a supply of recruits of this stamp from the counties, anything that the novelist has described could easily be paralleled.

5. A BUCCANEERING PHYSICIAN.

Amongst the irregular products of our University system Thomas Dover certainly deserves some recognition. His title is a three-fold one. As the inventor of the "powder," he must be still familiar to the childish stomach, or to those who have the control of it. As an adventurous leader in a daring privateering,— one might almost say buccaneering,—voyage round the world, he greatly distinguished himself. Finally, though not "the only begetter" of Robinson Crusoe, he was at least an indirect progenitor of that famous solitary, for he was the actual discoverer of Alexander Selkirk on the Island of Juan Fernandez.

Cambridge cannot claim the monopoly of Thomas Dover, so far as his early education is concerned. He came to us from Oxford, where he had spent some years, and had graduated in arts at St. Mary's Hall. Apparently it was the medical reputation of Caius College which attracted him, for he resided some time with us and took his M.B. in 1687. From our matriculation register, and other sources, we learn that he was a son of Captain John Dover, gentleman, of Barton on Heath, Warwickshire, and that he was baptized May 6, 1662.

After obtaining his qualification here he seems for some years to have devoted himself to medical or surgical practice at Bristol. This great seaport was then, and had for long been, the starting point for some of the most adventurous expeditions in which British

M

sailors have ever indulged. Dover must have
lived in an atmosphere of narrative and rumour
about the wealth of dollars which by judicious
daring might be extracted from the pockets of
Spanish dons in the South Sea. And doubtless
he numbered amongst his patients not a few
who had been wounded in some desperate sea-
fight off the Spanish Main, or brought home
stricken with fever in some pestilential swamp
of South America. Prominent amongst the
names in the mouth of every Bristolian must
have been the name of William Dampier,
the famous buccaneer and circumnavigator.
Though not of Bristol, he was a Somerset
man, and had already distinguished himself
by three daring voyages.

Dover's first public appearance is in 1708.
England was then at war with both France and
Spain, and some of the worthy citizens of
Bristol saw their way to serving their own
country, or at least to filling their own pockets,
by fitting out a small expedition to prey upon
the Spanish towns and commerce on the West
Coast of America. Some twenty of them combined, of whom Dover seems to have been one
of the most important, from his stake in the
venture or his personal influence, as he is
called " President" of the party. Two ships
were fitted out, *The Duke* of 300 tons with 30
guns and 170 men, and *The Dutchess* of 270
tons, 26 guns, and 151 men. The articles of
agreement are fully given in the printed
accounts, these mostly dealing, as might be
expected, with the division of the prize-money,

or "plunder," as they frankly call it. Dover had not apparently any sea qualifications, but several good men were selected for command. Woodes Rogers, already known as an explorer, was first captain of the *Duke*, Dover being called "second captain." Edward Cooke, also an experienced man, commanded the *Dutchess*, whilst the famous Dampier was "pilot" to the expedition, as being already familiar with places to which they proposed to go.

What strikes the modern reader is the almost incredible recklessness of the whole procedure. The smallness of their vessels may of course be taken for granted: the great Captain Cook, 50 years later, started in a ship not very much greater than the *Duke*. They knew almost nothing of the seas into which they were to penetrate. The position of Juan Fernandez, one of the places at which they were to call, was doubtful within several degrees of latitude and longitude. The Spaniards had been in nearly exclusive possession for two centuries, the seas swarmed with their ships, and the towns they proposed to attack were mostly fortified. They had few or no charts, and for such information as they could procure they mostly had to trust to catching a Spanish ship and taking their sailing directions from them. As to the crews who were to navigate these ships the following is the description given by their own captain: "many were taylors, tinkers, pedlars, fiddlers, and hay-makers, with ten boys and one negro; with which mixed gang we hope to be well manned as soon as they have learnt the use of arms, and got their sea legs." As to their cleanliness we have an indication during the customary "crossing the line" ceremony. It was the practice to hoist the novices half-way to a yard-arm and drop them into the sea. "This proved of great use to our fresh-water sailors, to recover the colour of their skins, which were grown very black and nasty." Throughout the voyage the crew—as was said to be common with these privateers — were in a state of suppressed or open mutiny. They had barely reached the Bay of Biscay when, seeing a strange sail, they pursued and overtook it. As it proved to be from Sweden, a country with which England was not at war, it was let go. The crew at once mutinied, because they were not allowed to plunder the ship; "while I (Captain Rogers), was on board the Swede, our men mutinyed; the ringleaders being our boatswain and three inferior officers." The revolt was suppressed and the leaders put in irons. Some time after, Rogers notes, "a sailor followed by near half the ship's company came aft to the steeridge door, and demanded the boatswain out of irons." So they went on during most of the voyage. The only resource of the captains, was, that when a seaman became too insolent to them or too friendly with his fellows they sent him from one ship to the other. Sometimes a large portion of the crew were thus shuffled. An occasional resource seems to have been to make one mutineer flog another, "which method," says Rogers, "I

thought best for breaking any unlawful friendship amongst themselves." And yet, somehow,
with traditional luck and pluck, they muddled
through. They circumnavigated the world in
a more than three years' voyage. They braved
the terrors of Cape Horn; they stormed a fortified city; they took many prizes; they crossed
the vast expanse of the Pacific,—during nearly
two months they did not apparently sight a
ship or an island;—and they reached home
with both their ships and much the greater part
of their crew. One point deserves notice. The
sickness on board was very slight for those days.
It was indeed insignificant when compared
with that which befell Lord Anson's similar
expedition which was fitted out at national
expense, and regularly commissioned, some 30
years later; but then Anson does not seem to
have taken the precaution of securing the
services of a Cambridge M.B.

Dover's actual position in the expedition is
not clearly defined, but there can be no doubt
that he was one of the leaders. At the same
time, though they had ordinary surgeons on
board, he seems to have been always appealed to
in case of emergency. As may be supposed, considering the times and the sort of crew with
whom he had to deal, his methods were not of
the mildest. At Quayaquil they encamped near
a mass of putrefying corpses, and some days
afterwards, when they were at sea, what seems
like an attack of plague broke out on board. He
dealt with the patients as follows: "I ordered
the surgeons to bleed them in both arms,—(the

patients were over 180 in number),—and to go round to them all, with command to leave them bleeding, till all were blooded, and then come and tie them up in their turns. Thus they lay, bleeding and fainting so long that I could not conceive they could have lost less than an hundred ounces each man." According to him this treatment was completely successful. He lost only seven or eight of the whole number, and these he says perished because their messmates would dose them with rum.

We have two detailed accounts of the expedition, one by Captain Rogers, and the other by Captain Cooke, which, like all these first-hand narratives, are of extreme interest; but there is only space here to describe one or two incidents, in which Dover took a prominent part.

After the customary difficulties in rounding Cape Horn, during which they got as far south as nearly 62°, "which, for aught we know is the furthest that anyone has yet been to the southward," and after considerable perplexity as to the exact position of Juan Fernandez, they at last hit that island on the morning of Jan. 31, 1709. A light being seen on the island they had some suspicions that a French or Spanish party might be there. Accordingly Dover, with a small armed body of sailors landed in order to reconnoitre. The result was "our pinnace returned from the shore, and brought abundance of crawfish, with a man cloth'd in goat-skins, who looked wilder than the first owners of them. He had been on the island four years and four months. . . . His name was Alexander

ACADEMIC "SPORTS"   167

Selkirk." Thence Robinson Crusoe; though, as
is well known, Defoe placed his hero on the
opposite side of America, near the mouth of the
Orinoco[1].

After spending some time at Juan Fernandez,
in order to recover from the hardships of their
passage round the Horn, Dover and his companions set to work on their real business, the
plunder of the Spaniard. "In the hopes of
seeing rich ships either going or coming out of
Lima: the men beginning to repine that, tho
come so far, we have met with no prizes in
these seas." We find such entries as these in
Captain Cooke's journal: "Our prisoners informed us that a Bishop was coming by sea
from Panama to Lima, carrying 200,000 pieces of
eight and a good quantity of plate of his own."
He directs one small ship "to cruise with 30
men for the Bishop above mentioned." But his
lordship, unfortunately, caught the alarm and
stayed on shore. In what was doubtless the
great object of their ambition, that which had
fired the imagination of buccaneers, privateers,
and regular service men for a century, they did
not succeed. They could not catch one of the

---

[1] Juan Fernandez was at that time entirely uninhabited,
and only visited at rare intervals by Spanish ships. It lies
more than 200 miles off the coast of Chile. Several characteristics of the Island life are reproduced in Crusoe, for
instance the presence of goats, and Selkirk's activity in
running them down. But there was one detail which must
have struck Defoe's fancy, though such a stickler for apparent
truth could not introduce it into fiction. The island swarmed
so with *cats* that they were a main article of diet. Shelvocke,
a few years later, reports "they are so numerous there is
hardly taking a step without starting one." Some passing
ship had once left a pair there.

great Spanish galleons which annually crossed the Pacific from Acapulco on the (now) Californian coast to the Phillipines, loaded with gold and silver. They had not the luck of Drake, Dampier, or Anson. But they did not do badly on the whole. They picked up a number of unconsidered trifles, in the way of coasting vessels, each affording its share of plunder; and they made two more serious attempts on what were called "Manilla ships." These seem to have been the vessels which brought supplies from the East Indies—the Phillipines, etc.—to the towns on the West coast of America. They were poor spoil in comparison with those which sailed the other way, carrying back the treasure from the mines of Peru and Mexico, but they were well worth incurring some risk. The first of these which they attacked was taken with little trouble or loss, as it was only of about the strength of one of their own. With the second they were less successful. It was a ship of 900 tons, with 60 guns, and a crew of 450, and their total available strength was under 120 men. Moreover their largest round shot were six-pounders, which, as they say, did very little damage to the galleon. After a long and desperate engagement, and repeated attempts to board, they were obliged to bear off, having lost a number of men, and with their captain, Rogers, badly wounded.

Their principal exploit in the South Seas was unquestionably the capture of Guayaquil, an important Spanish town in what is now Ecuador. In this, Dover took a prominent part; in fact, if we were to trust his own words written late in life—"when I took by storm the two cities of Guaiquil"—we should have to conclude that he was sole leader. On the other hand, Rogers considered that Dover nearly spoilt their chances by advocating delay when they found that the town was alarmed. "Captain Dover, the doctor of physic"—the seaman is fond of a gibe at the physician—"and he fell into a debate of above an hour as to whether to attack the place then in the dark during this first alarm or not." The majority decided for delay. A ransom of 40,000 dollars was proposed at first; but finding that the Spaniards were using the delay to carry off their plate and jewels into the forest, they proceeded to attack. The result was what it generally was when a party of these desperadoes fell upon a fortified Spanish city. They took it at once by storm, with insignificant loss. In fact they had but two men wounded, and one of these by their own fire. They then proceeded to get what they could in the way of plunder, in which respect they seem to have done fairly well, for two young officers "brought back with them gold chains, plate, &c., to the value of over £1,000." Having taken the city they recommenced the dispute about the ransom. The Spaniards offered to pay 30,000 dollars in 12 days, but, suspecting them of a design to send to neighbouring cities for succour, the Englishmen declared that "they would see the town all on fire by three that afternoon unless they agreed to give sufficient hostages for the money to be paid within six days." This was agreed to; and the party left the town, grumbling much at the thought of how much more they might have had but for the misjudged delay in assaulting the town. "I was well assured from all hands," says Rogers, "that at least we should then have got above 200,000 pieces of eight (*i.e.* dollars) in money, and a greater plenty of such necessaries as we now found." The terms of agreement are duly given in Rogers' narrative. "Whereas the City of Guiaquil, lately in subjection to Philip V, King of Spain, is now taken by storm and in the possession of Captains Thomas Dover, Woodes Rogers, and Stephen Courtney, commanding a body of Her Majesty of Great Britain's subjects, &c., &c."

After leaving Guayaquil they cruised about off the American coast for nearly nine months in the hope of securing one of the great Manilla galleons. In this, as already stated, they were only partially successful. But they picked up a number of small prizes, one of which was converted into a third cruiser, and put under the command of Dover. The selection of a commander by the vote of the majority of those under him seems to have been a common practice in these semi-buccaneering expeditions. Rogers strongly objected to the choice, his objection being "that owing to his violent temper capable men could not well act under him, while as a Dr. of Physick he was incapable as a seaman himself."

At last, on the 11th of January, 1710, they started to cross the Pacific. On the parallel of latitude they took, the distance to the first

land they seem to have sighted was between
6000 and 7000 miles. They had no charts;
had they met any other vessel it would certainly
have been a hostile one; and one of their small
ships was so leaky that the pumps had to be
constantly at work, "which labour, together
with being on short allowance, makes our
people look miserably." We can well believe it.

After two months of this lonely voyage
they reached Guan, one of the Ladrones:
islands which are now in possession of
Germany but then belonged to Spain. It is
an extraordinary illustration of the free and
easy way in which war was then made in the
remote regions of the world that whereas on
the Eastern parts of the Pacific they had been
in constant and deadly warfare with the
Spaniards, they found it convenient to adopt
a different plan on approaching the Western
parts. They mustered up their best knowledge
of the language and sent a "civil request" to
the Governor of the island, to the effect that
"we being servants of her Majesty of Great
Britain, stopping at these islands on our way
to the East Indies"—a rather odd statement
of the main object of the expedition—"will
not molest the settlement provided you deal
friendly with us, &c." No objections were
raised by the Spaniards, who at once sent them
some much-needed supplies, so that, as Rogers
says, "being now arrived at a place of peace and
plenty we all became indifferent well reconciled
among ourselves." In fact so friendly did the
relations become that the privateers invited the

Governor and a party of Spanish gentlemen to
an entertainment on board one of the ships,
"where we all met and made them as welcome
as time and place would afford, with music and
our sailors dancing." Probably all the time the
guests had a shrewd suspicion as to the cargo on
board, which their hosts had picked up "on
their way to the East Indies."

After thoroughly enjoying themselves at
Guan they started homewards by way of
Batavia. Hereabouts, on the 17th of June,
1710, they met the first ship bound from Europe
since they started from Bristol in August, 1708.
From her they learnt, amongst other facts of
interest, that England was still at war. After
another three months' voyage, and encounter-
ing innumerable dangers and hardships, they
brought their leaky ships to Cape Town: "the
Duke having three feet of water in her, and her
pumps choked." There they delayed for nearly
three months, and at last set sail for home:
this time in company with a number of Dutch
East Indiamen and several English ships.
They approached England by way of the West
Coast of Ireland and the Shetland Isles—presumably to avoid hostile cruisers—and reached
the Thames, October 14th, 1711.

How far the expedition was successful
pecuniarily, we do now know; but for certain
hints by subsequent adventurers we should
conclude that it led to much dispute and disappointment.

After his return Dover seems to have settled
down to a professional life in England. Though

he never proceeded to M.D. he obtained recognition from the College of Physicians, and practised in various parts of the country. It may be well supposed that a man of his character and antecedents was not likely to lead a strictly conventional life. In fact he seems to have been in constant disputes with the regular physicians. What we know of his after life is mainly derived from his *Ancient physician's Legacy to his country*, of which the sixth edition appeared when he was nearly 80. It belongs to the class of The Family Doctor rather than to that of the professional treatise, and abounds with such personalities as this: "The case of Miss Corbet was so very remarkable that it made a very great noise all over the town, insomuch that the gentlemen of the faculty seemed to be much alarmed. The Right Honourable and Lady Louisa Berkeley, being left off by other physicians; and the Right Honourable the Lady Rachel Manners being likewise left off by her physicians, it was agreed on all hands that I kept them alive several days longer than was expected by any person about." These were some of his few admitted failures. In other cases he describes minutely the symptoms of patients whose names and addresses he gives.

He was generally known by the name of the "Quick-silver doctor," from his fondness for prescribing this drug. The following is his recipe for Asthma: "In the removing of this disease, I don't remember an instance of my failing in the cure of any person who has

applied to me for relief. I make use of this easy
remedy : An ounce of quicksilver every day, to
be taken at what hour the patient pleases and
a spoonful of the gas of sulphur in a large
draught of spring water at five o'clock and at
bed-time." As it happens, his "Powder,"—
which Dr. Norman Moore tells me is still
substantially the same composition as that
which Dover prescribed—is all by which his
name is now generally known. When and
where he ended his varied and adventurous life
I have not been able to discover.

(Since the above was written some further
facts have been ascertained. It seems he was
buried at Stanway, Gloucs., Ap. 15, 1742. For
this, and other family facts I am indebted to
Dr. J. A. Nixon. See his account in the *Bristol
Med. and Chir. Journal*, March, 1909.)

6. A Barbary Slave.

*A Modest Vindication of Titus Oates, the Salamanca Doctor,
from Perjury : Or an Essay to Demonstrate him only
forsworn in several Instances. By Adam Elliott, M.A.,
1682.*

Such is the title of a pamphlet which
contains much matter of interest—not merely
to readers of a College magazine, in consequence
of the local connections of the two persons
principally concerned in it—but to all who are
interested in the social and political history of
the time ; in which respect it would be difficult
to find any more graphic description of the

perils which stood in the way of travellers
by sea in former days.

The immediate object of the work—which it
must be remembered was published several
years before Oates' judicial condemnation, and
at a time when he was still in great popular
repute—was to cleanse the author's character
from some splashes of the filth which Oates
had been casting upon so many of those who
had the ill-fortune to come within reach of his
shovel. Elliott was charged with being "a
Mahumetan, and thereupon circumcised"; and
also with being a Jesuit and a Popish priest.
On this latter charge, as a capital one, Elliott
remarks: "I must indeed confess that of all
kinds of death I have the least fondness to be
hanged, and I hate mortally that the butcherly
Executioner should be rummaging amongst
my Entrailes; neither can I apprehend any
pleasure in being drawn up Holborn Hill upon
a hurdle." In addition to the more serious
charges, Oates declared that he had known
Elliott as a bad subject since their College
days, when "the sayd Elliott robbed a study
in Caius, and would have sold the deponent
some of the books; that he hath confessed
that he went a deer-stealing"; and that he was
a sizar "whose maintenance was withdrawn
for his rude, riotous and debauched living,
etc., etc."

To all this Elliott—very sensibly remarking,
"I had rather the Doctor should swing than I"
—replies with a counter-statement of some of
Oates' perjuries, and with a brief narrative of

his own life and adventures during the time in question. The following pages are extracts made from this narrative :—

"In the year 1664 I was admitted into Caius Colledge where I continued until 1668; when Commencing Batchlour of Arts I obtained Letters testimonial from our Colledge, and then left the University. During my stay there, I remember Titus Oates was entered; by the same token that the *Plague* and *he* both visited the University in the same year. He was very remarkable for a Canting Fanatical way conveyed to him with his Anabaptistical Education, and in our Academical exercises, when others declaimed Oates always preached; some of which lectures, they were so very strange that I do yet remember them.

"In the beginning of 1669 I had the opportunity of travelling with some gentlemen of my acquaintance, with whom, after a transient view of Flanders, which had been the seat of war for some years preceding, I had the opportunity to see St. Omers also, where Oates was once a school-boy. I remember, during my stay there, we were civilly invited to dinner to the English Colledge ; where, to give the Devil his due, we met with nothing but learning and civility. About November we came to Rome; where I saw that Great Beast of a Whore, as Oates called him, a Reverend old Gentleman Rospigliosi who then was Pope. He happened to die a little after my coming thither, which was the occasion of my fortune to stay here during the election of another Pope.

"About March, 1670, I parted from Rome; and intending home again for England I came to Leghorn, where finding an opportunity of the *Bristol*, one of His Majesty's Friggots, I had a convenient passage to Alicante in Spain, and from thence to Malaga. About the beginning of May I had a curiosity to see Seville; from whence I took my course directly to Lisbon. There was at that time no vessel designed for England in the river of Lisbon, excepting a little Ketch called the *John of London*, laden with oranges and lemons, and I was very desirous to return home; so that I was obliged to take my passage in that small vessel, some who seconded my desires alledging that I should be more secure in her than in a bigger, because she by reason of her smallness would keep near the Coast and so out of danger of the Turks. It was about the middle of June, 1670. Three days after that we met Sir Edward Sprag with his squadron, who encouraged us with the news that no pirats were in those seas, he having lain there about a month; upon which we struck out to sea. By the 22nd of June we had got no farther than Cape Finisterre; on which day, whilst the master and I were at breakfast, a Boy who sat at the Helm cried out a Sail. By our Glasses we perceived she had a mind to speak with us, for she had got out all her sails and bore down upon us directly before the wind. About ten a-clock up comes the Ship with *French* colours: as soon as she came near us, so that we could not escape, she pulled down her French and put up her *Salle* colours, and

N

withall gave us a Gun which obliged us to strike.[1] Immediately appeared upon the Pirat's deck about 200 Moors, who commanded us to put out our Boat and come aboard them. For our welcome, and to show what entertainment we were after to expect, the Master of the Vessel and myself were stripped and tyed to the mast in order to be whipped, that so they might extort a confession where the Money lay hid, if we had any. We satisfied them that they were Masters of all in our Vessel; and so we were released from the Mast and put in Irons below deck. Our cruel and merciless Masters, when they heard us complain of our condition, would visit us with blows, insulting most intolerably over us, lifting up our dejected heads and spitting upon our Faces, not vouch-safing us any other Name than Dogs.

"We lay in this miserable condition about forty days, oppressed with many inconven-iences, so especially I remember with the stench of our lodging. Sometimes in the day we were permitted to come above deck, to suck in a little fresh air, and to wash ourselves; but this small comfort was soon forgot by returning to our irons. There was scarce a day almost, accord-ing to my remembrance, in which we did not either give chase or else were chased; for the Salle man was a good sailor and whenever she saw a Sail she immediately made after her; if she found her too strong to grapple with, then

---

[1] The student of History will remember that it was by a " Sallee Rover ", a few years before this date, that Robinson Crusoe was captured.

she tacked and stood away. At length one
morning, when there was little wind stirring,
we were called up upon the Deck, I thought it
had been to refresh ourselves, but we found it
was with labour and toil, for there being a great
calm all that day, we were obliged to tug hard
at the oar till ten at night; at which time we
came up with a French Merchant laden with
oyl, whom we had been in pursuit of all that
day. As soon as we came near her, we poor
Christians were remanded to our kennel. A
little after, three and twenty Frenchmen had
the unhappiness to make us a visit, and take up
their lodgings in the same quarters. It was but
a miserable comfort methought to have such
companions in misery, and truly the sight of so
many dejected souls, particularly a merchant
(who lost 2500 crowns of cash, besides his
concerns in the cargo) affected me then with a
more sensible grief than my own sufferings.
We were all lodged equally; that French
gentleman and the meanest of the seamen were
treated alike: which subjected him to such a
grief that was too powerful for him, so that at
length it broke his heart, for he died the next
day after we landed.

"At length we came within sight of the
Castle of Salle. Presently there starts up a
vessel that made all the sail she could at us,
and obliged us to tack about and strike down
along the Barbary Coast. She put us so hard
to it that we were forced to forsake the
French Prize and leave her to be picked up
by our pursuer, which was an English ship

called the *Holmes* Frigot, of two-and-twenty guns, whom afterwards I saw at my return at Cales. Whilst she was employed in taking the prize the Salleman in the interim made away, and night approaching, in the dark made her escape.

"The next morning all we Christians were commanded a-shoar. There they landed us in number two-and-thirty. We were above two days travelling the twenty leagues. The best water we met with was very brackish; our provision which our Masters allowed us, when we parted from the ship was all devoured the first day. Our condition indeed during that journey was the most deplorable that ever I was in; for our short commons and hard lodging aboard the Ship had much weakened our bodies; we were very hungry and had no meat, exceeding thirsty and for a whole day no water, the Sun was very hot and no shelter, the Heavens looked like brass and the Earth like iron. When night approached our Guides made us take up our lodging where there were a few shrubs which we set on fire to secure us from the lions and other beasts of prey, as Wild Boars, of which we saw several on our way.

"At length upon the third day we came within sight of Salle, where we were permitted to refresh ourselves for two hours before we made our public entry into the City, which was indeed extraordinary; for we were accompanied by several hundreds of idle rascally people and roguish boys who came

out of the town to meet us and welcomed
us with horrid barbarous shouts somewhat
like the *Irish hubbub*. We in the mean time
were forced like a drove of sheep through the
several streets, the people crowding to gaze
upon us and curse us. At evening we were
conveyed to our Lodgings. It was a large Cellar
under the Street, arched and supported with
two rows of pillars; the light it was furnished
with came through three holes in the street
strongly grated, through one of which by a
Ladder of Ropes, we descended into this Room
called the King's *Masmora*, capacious enough
to hold 300 persons (for very near that number
of Christians were shut up there at night)
besides a whole Leystall of filth, in which
(whosoever's lot it is to be there) he must
wade up to the ancles. There I watched all
night, for sleep I could not.

"By Sun-rising next morning we were driven
to a Market-place where the Moors sitting
Taylor-wise upon Stalls round about, we were
severally run up and down by persons who
proclaimed our qualities or trades. I had a
great Black who was appointed to sell me.
this fellow, holding me by the hand, coursed
me up and down from one person to another
to examine me what trade I was of, and to
see what labour my hands were acccustomed
to. All the seamen were soon bought up, it
was mid-day ere I could meet with a purchaser;
the reason was, a boy of the vessel wherein I
was taken, in hopes of favourable treatment
from the Captain who took us, pretended to

discover my quality to him, assuring him that I was a relation of the now Duke of Norfolk. Upon this information the Captain put a great value upon me, and that was the reason why none would meddle with me; until about noon Hamed Lucas (who is secretary of the present embassy from the Emperor of Fez to his Majesty) paid down 600 pieces of Eight for me.

"I was pretty well pleased with my fortune to fall into the hands of such a person, and hoped for favourable treatment from him; but other Christians who had heard of this patron of mine pitied my ignorance, as knowing that he was a cunning Jewish Merchant, and that he bought me with a design to extort from me a great Ransome, though by the harshest and cruellest usage imaginable. This I found to be too true a character of him before night; for after he was come to his own house he presently makes me acquainted with a piece of his mind and temper telling me that he would have me know that I had to do with a man with a *beard*, and who was too cunning to be imposed upon. I endeavoured all I could to disabuse him, and possess him with a clear notion of the naked truth in regard to my poverty; that I should very much contribute to the calling in question his prudence and judgment, because all the town will admire that the wise Hamet Lucas was imposed upon in giving 600 pieces of Eight for a poor Slave who was not worth a maravidi. At which words he was so transported with passion that he showered down a whole torrent of blows upon me, and lighting unluckily upon a stick, he broke my head in several places, and never ceased until he had made me all in a gore-blood. I was not able to stir, and the cruel villain permitted me to lie a little while; afterwards he comes again afresh, and drags me out of his House into the Streets, and then falls upon me anew, beating me all along the Streets. He brought me at length to a Black-Moor who was working in Lime, commanding me with all cruel imperious insolence to serve that Black by giving up lime with my hands, which I did till such time as my Patron departed; and then I signified to the Black that I was very sick, and by signs prayed him to let me leave off that work which had almost choked me; which by his gesture I perceived he allowed. So I lay down upon the ground and fell asleep; my Patron presently returned, and took such a course to awake me that he had very nearly laid me asleep for ever; for he gave me a blow in the small of my back which created such a pungent pain as quite cashiered all patience and all respects of self-preservation.

"The next day he provided a Jew, who had been in Europe and spoke good Latin, to treat with me, as if my defect in the Castilian language had occasioned the unsuccessfulness of his negotiating with me. This Jew I found to be a good understanding man, endowed with more humanity than generally the people of that religion are, which he evidenced by his good advice to me, telling me that my patron

was a man of violent passions, and that though
he himself was pretty well satisfied of my utter
inability, yet if my Patron should be so
persuaded and find himself bilked in all his
great expectations, he would certainly convert
his hopes into an extravagant rage, and then
put me to some cruel death. Therefore he
advised me, as not to sooth his vain hopes, so
neither quite to banish them. You shall give
me leave, says he, to acquaint your Patron that
you have Relations and Friends who are powerful and rich; that rather than you should
spend all your days under the pressure of a
heavy and cruel Captivity they would make a
purse of 1,000 Crowns to ransome you.

"The Christians, usually about Sun-setting,
were sent to a fountain without the town, to
bring home in great earthern Jars some of that
water. I also was sent by my patron. Amongst
other discourse I listened to a seaman speaking
of Mamora, a Spanish garrison, some twenty
miles distant from Salle; and that he, sailing
along the coast had observed it very rocky for
about eight miles, but the next was a fine sand.
He said, moreover, that he believed a good foot-
man might run a race for his freedom in three
hours, if he had the convenience of a favourable
night and could scape a number of Tents which
were pitched all along the country betwixt Salle
and Mamora, who are very industrious to pick
up slaves attempting an escape, Upon this
discourse it entered strongly into my head that
I should be the person who should win this
prize; but at present it was impossible by

reason of my lodging in the *Masmora*, as also
by reason of my lassitude at night being quite
spent with the toil of the day. But if I could
induce my Patron by any arts to be a little kind
to me and abate his severity I thought I might
fall into some capacity of performing what I
designed.

"(The sequel is too long to relate in full.
But, after some time, he so far ingratiated
himself that at supper one evening, after waiting
on the company, he was asked to sit down
and join them. Though they were mostly
Mahometans there was no stint of wine.)

"After these compliments were over I sat
down with the company and composed myself
to be as merry and agreeable as possibly I
could. I sung several English songs to them,
particularly I remember, "Calm was the Evening, etc.," in the *Mock Astrologer*, which was
new when I left England. They were wonder-
fully affected with it, and were very desirous
to have me translate ha, ha, ha, etc., into
Spanish. They also sung to requite me. I
must confess I never knew any who seemed
much diverted with the sweetness of my voice,
but really when I heard their barbarous Tones
and damnable dissonant Jangling, I cannot
deny a piece of weakness which then possessed
me, which was a pleasure to hear my own sweet
self chant it. The glass in the meanwhile did
not stand still. Though I used all art to shift
it from myself yet I used the same that my
Patron might never balk it; which at last
evidenced itself plainly, for he was got very

drunk, and truly I thought that then it was not safe nor convenient to my purposes for his Slave to appear sober. Therefore I counterfeited the humours of a man overtaken with drink, so that I afforded exceeding divertisement to the soberer part of the Company. Before midnight all the Company had got as much as they could well carry away, and my Patron abundance more.

"Seeing that my Patron was engaged in a deep sleep, from which he would not awake in four or five hours, I took out of his bags a small parcel of Spanish Pistols (pistoles), which methought might not be unserviceable to me in another part of the world, together with two shirts of his (for, indeed, I had none of my own), and a pair of shoes; I put out the Candles and with all expedition I slipt out of a window into the street, where I unsheathed my sword, being resolved to attack whomsoever I should rencounter in the streets. I came at last to the Riverside, near the Castle, where presently I threw myself in, but after having been a little there, finding myself incommoded in swimming by reason of the Sword and other things, I swum back to shoar, where I stripped myself and laid all upon my back kept together by my breeches buttoned about my neck. But my proceeding was slow by reason of the burden I carried, and my arms were weary. Whereupon I unbuttond and let all my clothes, riches and armour go together, and swimming on my back I at length came to the other side of the River, a little weary, and altogether naked and defenceless.

"Now the dangers began to crowd upon me, and I had so near a prospect of them that I wished I had never undertook the work; but when I reflected on the loss of my Patron's scimitar and the Gold, my desperate estate gave me both hopes and courage. So up I got, and having almost rounded North Salle, with a good speed I made away, having no other direction saving the noise of the breaking of the Sea upon the Shoar on my left hand. It was dark, and there was no path or road, so that many times I stumbled and fell over stones, which cut and bruised my naked body. Towards day-break I turned to the left over a great Bank, on the other side of which I happily fell in upon a sand which continued about eleven or twelve miles in length, where I exercised my feet to the best purpose that ever 1 think I did in my life, and then I came within sight of Mamora the Spanish Garison, I called out to them that I was a Christian, and begged them to relieve me. They waved their hats to me, and looking behind I saw the Moors coming down upon me; then I made all the haste that fear could inspire me with, the Spaniards in the mean time firing at the Moors to stop their eager pursuit. At last with my utmost endeavours I reached the little Fort at the bottom of which I fell down quite spent. The Soldiers carried me up in a Cloak to the Garison, where the Governour, after having caused a glass of wine to be poured into my mouth to revive me, questioned me what I was and whence I came (for indeed I was so covered all over my body with blood, sweat and dust, that it was hard to distinguish me from a Moor by my colour) I satisfied him that I was an Englishman whom God had been so merciful to as last night to bestow an opportunity of escaping from a heavy slavery at Salle. By noon the Moors being within reach of the guns the Governour commanded to let fly among them; and I, upon my request to honour my Patron (who was among them) had the favour to fire two, so that they made haste to be gone.

"It is hard to be expressed what a great satisfaction it was to me to see my cruel enemy (whom but 24 hours before I dreaded as the Indians do the Devil) flee from me and endeavour an escape out of my reach with as much eagerness as the night before I did out of his. Yet when I reflected upon the weakness of the Garison which was no bigger in circumference than the Tower of London; the feeble resistance that 400 disheartened half-starved sickly Spaniards could make against an innumerable swarm of Moors, I must confess my fears did a little qualify my joy and I could not forbear wishing that my Patron and I were at a greater distance.

"The next morning early, five Barca-Longo's, which had brought provision from Cadiz, were returning home, in one of which I gladly embarked, bidding adieu to Mamora (which since about two years ago, as I heard with sorrow) was taken by the Moors after above 100 years possession of the Spaniards. Hamet Lucas being the first man who entered it.

"Upon Wednesday morning we were got far as A-lanach, another Garrison belonging to the Spaniards, at which time we heard much shooting out at sea, so that we thought it convenient to put in. The town is fortified by two strong Castles, well stored with great Ordnance, into one of which we were permitted to ascend to view a rare sight: a very unequal combat yet briskly maintained by one Dutch man-of-war against six Algerines. The fight continued until noon, when two great Dutch men-of-war coming up, the Turks thought best to make sail and stand away. Then luckily, 'ahead of them as they were weathering Cape Spartil, appeared six English men-of-war. The Algerines being hemmed in resolved rather to venture through the English. But Captain Beach, with the first broadside disabling their Admiral, they altogether tacked and ran ashore in the Bay of Arzilla, where they were all set on fire, abundance of Christians being relieved and abundance of Turks being killed.

"Next day being Thursday, we set forward for Cadiz. There I saw some of those very Moor slaves themselves who made me so; there being 15 taken aboard the French prize I formerly mentioned, by the *Holmes* Frigot, and carried to Cadiz and there sold. This gave me a pleasant opportunity of thinking how the case was altered. The agent prevailed with the Dutch Consul to grant me passage for England in a Dutch *Man-of-War* (there being no English ships of any force then in the River, and I was very unwilling any more to hazard myself

in small vessels). It was the very same ship
which I saw at Alanache engaged with the six
Algerines.   In the beginning of November I was
brought to the Texel, having had no convenience to be removed into any ship in the
channel by reason of a great storm that hurried
us over to the Holland Coast. From Amsterdam
I came to the Hague, where hearing that Sir
John Chicheley, then envoy from his Majesty to
the Governour of the Spanish Netherlands, was
returning for England, I made haste to Brussels
and obtained passage for England amongst his
retinue."

(Elliott's subsequent experiences seem to
have been of a more commonplace character.
He became rector of a London parish, St. James,
Duke place, in 1685.   He died about the beginning of the year 1700, having been suspended
from his parish for part of the time for irregular
performance of marriages.)

XI.

UNDERGRADUATE LETTERS OF THE 17TH CENTURY.

The members of the Gawdy family, one of whose principal seats was at West Harling in Norfolk, seem to have been, like the Pastons of the same county, great letter writers. There is a large collection at the British Museum, known as the Gawdy MSS., which contains many hundreds of letters written to and from various members of the family. Though far from rivalling the famous find of Sir John Fenn in respect of antiquity, many of them are old enough to be of much value. The following are selected from the correspondence of the junior members of the family, the writers being students at Cambridge. The Gawdys belonged to the country gentry, and occupied, if not the highest place, at any rate a dignified and substantial place in the county. In the early part of the seventeenth century, Framlingham Gawdy, Esquire of West Harling, was a prosperous landowner with a large family. No less than six of his sons came successively to College. It deserves notice that only one of them proceeded to a degree. Modern sentiment on the subject would regard this as representing somewhat of a failure, suggesting, presumably, idleness or want of ability. But it was entirely in accordance with the sentiment of the time. It is often forgotten that the society in College in those days consisted of two really distinct classes, who may be described as the professional and the amateur, and who probably associated very little with each other. The former comprised the sizars—a rather numerous body at that time—and the scholars. These came with a distinctly professional end in view—to take a degree, and in most cases to become clergymen. Many of these, of course, had a very hard struggle here, and for them such amusements as those which bulk so largely in modern collegiate life, were quite out of the question. The other class comprised many of the pensioners, and most of the fellow-commoners. If they looked forward to a profession it would either be that of the Law, or possibly that of the Church, with a family living securely awaiting them. The elder sons naturally settled down on their estates, and followed the duties expected of landed gentry. Most of the men of this class — with the exception of the few clergy—treated the College life as an episode in their general training for social life; from College, after a year or two of a certain amount of study, they probably went to an Inn of Court to get a smattering of Law. And then, if they could afford it, and the times were peaceful, they might very likely get a year or two of foreign travel. It is a different view of academic training from that commonly entertained now, which sometimes almost amounts to the commercial estimate that he who quits the University without a degree is like one who leaves his money on the counter and omits to take away what he came to buy. But there is a good deal to be said for the older view, if wisely interpreted.

It may be remarked that there were then a number of tutors in every College, in fact almost every resident Fellow had pupils, these tutors being often personally known to the parents, and selected for that reason. Except in the case of the very rich the whole College accounts probably passed through the tutor's hands, the father lodging a sum of money with him at the beginning of term, and the pupil applying to his tutor for what he wanted from time to time. The diary of a tutor about this time—the well-known Joseph Mede of Christ's—has happened to survive, and gives a very clear account of the ordinary expenses of a student, and of the books which he read, or, at least, which he bought.

Anthony Gawdy, the writer of the first letters, was a poor relation of the squire of Harling by whose help he was apparently supported at College. He was probably a nephew or cousin. He took Holy Orders (as the reader might infer from his ornate rhetoric), and soon obtained preferment in the county.

"Sr this is to let you onderstand that my Tutor have given me a note of my expences for this halfe yere, wharein if it please you you may examing every perticular in this bille, at the first sight peradventure it may seeme more than you expected, yet if you observe the grate many of perticulars which ware not onely necessarie, but also convenient, makes up this

o

indifferent sum : if yor worship be desirous to know what hast I made in my Jorny coming up I will certifie you. I cam from yor house of the weddensdaie and I did ly at Newmarket that night, the next daie I was in Cambridge by XII of the cloke, and thus I rest, beseeching you to send up this mony very speedilie.

Yor poor kinsman

ANTHONY GAUDY.

To the right worpl
Mr. Framlingham Gaudy Esq.;
these be delivered."

"A note of Anthony Gaudy his expences from our Lady to Michaelmas 1626.

	li	s.	d.
Commons and Sizing his scholler-shipp deducted	2	17	9
Chamber-Rent		7	6
Laundresse		3	0
Taylor for clothes mending ...		3	4
Supp (Supper) moneys		5	0
Shoes 2 payre newe and once soaling		7	8
For Mr. Michels of ould debt ...	1	5	0
Summa Tot. ...	5	9	3

Ita testor Nathan. Dod."

Nathaniel Dod was a junior Fellow at this time. The "supper money" was an occasional extra to spend in a tavern, or in College, rooms, for something more luxurious than the very plain fare commonly provided. Gawdy's scholarship was worth some two or three pounds a year.

"Worthy Sr, to omit complements, which be but flayeshes of wit without wisdome, or like a vapore, which when it feles the virtue of the sun is of smale continuance, or like the lightninge which is noe soner set on fyre by the influence of the heavens, but it is extinct; soe likewise If I should strive violently to extracte somewhat, out of my obtuse braine, which mought challinge the title of witt, in my owne conceipt, yet I know when it should make his aperance before yor judicious sensure, it would be but dew against the sunn. The occation of troubling yor wor. at this time is this much. I sent a letter lately to Bury, where in I certified yor worship hough thinges goe with me, concerning my Tutors leaveing of us, likewaies some monies due unto him, the some 25s., which he hath left one to receive in his absence, one that takes it ill, that he hase not yet received it, considering, we are of no grater acquaintance, my other letter, will give you ample satisfaction, in the perticulares: since his departure I went and intreated one Mr. Dod to bare my name and to let me have things necessarie, whilest the quarter daie, he beinge one that bareth affection towerds me, answered me thus: I would be glad to doe you any curtisie that lyeth in me, but you knowe it as a matter of waieght which we undertake, and yor friends are al together unknowne unto me, but thus much I will doe, lett but your Cosin wright unto me, and certifie me that he will discharge the Collidge as he hath hearetofore, and I shall rest contented. I beseech you Sr,

let me heare from you, or wright to him verie
shortly, for, for a man to live in the Collidge
without a tutor is as much disgrace, as for one
of your servants when you have turned him
awaye to hange still abawght your house. I
could willingly break promise that is, that I
would not complement, but trulie if I did
thinke that all the flowers of rethoricke could
move you in this one poynte, I would trie to
make use of them, concerning a bedd, which is
so needfull, but calling to mind the nature of
the flint, that often knocking uppon it doeth
rather produce fier out of it to consume than
watter to comforte the thurstie traviller, in like
manner I have bine often knocking uppon this
poynte to sture and move yor worship, but as
yet I see noe streames of pittie ishue from you
to comforte me in this distresse I will sease
therefore, leste I provocke yor ire to burne
against me in displesure, for then I cannot live
an our, I meane well.

I have noe nuse to salute yor worship with
all, but this to tell you hough honorable and
bountifull, our gratious Chanceller delte with
us, in making us all excede in venison: there
was never a table but had a pastie on one daie,
and the fellowes one every daie al the weeks
after, Sr Walsowie (Wallsall) Mr of Bennitt
Coll, is dede, and as yet there is noe election.

Yor pore kinsman
ANTHONY GAWDY
(circa August 1, 1626)."

Most of the above letter explains itself. The
Chancellor of the University, referred to in the

last paragraph, was George Villiers, the famous
Duke of Buckingham, whose election a few
weeks before caused so much excitement in the
University. Need it be said that the "exceeding
in venison " is not to be taken in an aldermanic
sense? The students of that day were divided,
for the purpose of dinner and supper, into a
number of "messes"; one consisting of the
scholars, one of the bachelors, two or more of
the pensioners, and so on. The ordinary fare at
table, as already remarked, was very plain. But
there were many Feasts, and on these and such
like occasions, a certain sum was allotted to
each table or mess. These were called "exceed-
ings" or "sizings." What the Duke seems to
have done was to send a number of bucks from
his park and distribute them amongst all the
Colleges, where the shares were divided amongst
the various messes.

"Worthy Sr, my tutor have received the
money, he is very glad, and I for my parte,
returne thankes, and that is all, yet thanks
payeth noe debts saith the proverbe. I acknow-
lidge it to be true, but how soe ever, though
they will not paie the principale, yet I will
endeavour to paye sum interest by my loyall
love and service. As farre as I understand by
my carrier you are disposed to bewtowe a shute
upon me. I confess it is the time now when
nature doeth cloeth all hir cretures: the earth
with grase, as the cloeth, and with diversitye of
flowers as it were the triming or setting out of
the garment: besides if you would be pleased

to observe, in yor own yarde, you shall not see any creature but dame nature will afford him a new coete in summer; goe we a little higher and behowld the birdes of the aier, and yow shall see them in the springe drope down their feathers, as men cast off there oulde shuts, and then put on another. Not to trouble you I am not determined to com doune till after the commencement, because it is now our chuife time of arts and disputations, but if then you thinke it fitting to let mee come and waight upon you (with all my harte); in the mean time I shall make shuift, or if you be other wayes disposed, I think Robert Levall heath my measure, I am not growne since you did see me neyther in haith nor bigness, but only I hope to growe every daye more and more, by my pore indeavours, in to yor faviour.

Yor porre kinsman
ANTHONY GAWDY."

One is glad to know that Mr. Gawdy apparently obtained his new suit, if one may judge by the private account which follows, which seems in addition to the previous one.

"A note of my owne expences from Michalemas to Christmas 1626.

	li	s.	d.
For my table	3	0	0
For making my shute and laieing out for thinges thare unto belongeing with mending my owld cloethes thare is due unto my Taylor	1	0	0

Received of my Tutor for shooes
and stokens, barber, and other
thinges   necessarie,   and   to
bringe me downe   1   0   0
For my expected cominge down...   5   0

Summa total   ...   5li   2   6"

(The last item has been corrected, and, by
the addition, apparently halved.)

"Worthy Sr, As I understand, by the Carier,
my last letter was somewhat distastfull unto
you: I doe not knowe but I thinke thare is noe
man that doth petition more humbly then
myselve : I did never fall in to any sausie terms
with you or seemed to challinge any thinge at
yor hands as dew: for I know the contrarie, that
what soever you doe for me is merely out of
charitie, and by no constrainte : the occasion of
now trublinge you is to let you understand
that the halve yeare is fully expired, and the
man with whome I live doth dayly expecte
mony from me, and yet my Tutor hath dis-
charged parte of it, contribiting to his neces-
sities as occation served, he hath never received
any benefit by me for tuition, but onely as a
freind hath undertaken for me, and laide it out :
in a word (for feare I should be trublsome) as
he that was able to delineate whole Hercules by
the sighte of his footstep, Soe likewaies you
may gather my whole intente, in these few
words, which is that you would be pleased to
send up this monie, with as conveniente speed

as you can possible lest I make toe boulde with this my friend

Yor poor kinsman

ANTHONY GAWDY.

(Addressed)   To the right worshipful, Mr. Framlingham Gawdy Esqr and High Sheruf of Norfolke."

As I have said, Anthony Gawdy subsequently became a rector in Norfolk. One is curious to know whether his flowery style and insinuating advances towards his patron and relative, found their full scope in his addresses to his parishioners and his relations with his bishop. Unfortunately he has left no published sermons behind him. We are grieved to have to say that his final relations with the College authorities were to say the least of it, somewhat strained. The incident has been already described, in a letter from the College tutor (v. p. 116).

Most of the other letters are from one or other of the sons of Framlingham Gawdy. Several of them entered as fellow-commoners, and as already remarked, only one of the six proceeded to a Degree. It seems that they did not keep horses during their residence, but had them sent to Cambridge for the journey home of some 35 or 40 miles.

"Deer father in your last letter you were about our coming home, you saide you would send for us a week or a fortnight after the commencement: I desire you (if you please) let our horses come upon Wednesday being the 13

daie of this moneth. I doubt not but you have
heard howe the sicknes is at Botsham : I should
have given you notice of it before if my carrier
had not bin prest for a souldier. So with our
dutye unto you and craving your blessing I rest
        Your dutiful and obedient sonne
                        WILLIAM GAWDY.
Gon. Cai. Col.
    6 of July 1621."

" Deer father wee did expect you heer at Cambridge at your going to London. I was chosen
by the proctours to bee senior brother in the
Commencement house this yeare, which is a
place of great credite, but withall very chargeable, for I should have given the proctours each
of them a sattin doublet and should have invited all the doctors and chiefe men in the
towne to supper : my tutor tooke some time to
consider of it, hopeing you would have come
this way, but you comming not I was con-
strained to refuse it. I desire you (if you buy a
newe hat before Easter) to bring downe mine
ready trimmed with you, for my ole one be-
ginnes to growe unfitting for a gentleman to
weare, and I am lothe to buy mee a new one
because it will not be long ere I shall have that
I pray let it be new shagged thoughe it bee
somewhat the thinner and (if it be possible) let
it bee made lesse in the heade, and let the
brimmes bee cut somewhat narrower as the
fashion is : and I pray let mee have a silver
girdle of the best sort, and let Frank Gaudy
bring it with him when you come into the

country at Easter, and I will pay you for it
againe. I pray you let me receive your letter
the next weeke by the Cambridge carrier. So
with my duty remembered unto you craving
your blessing and hoping to meet you at Harling a fortnight before Easter I rest

Your dutifull sonne

WILLIAM GAWDY.

From my study in Gon. & Cai. Col.
13th Nov., 1631."

The reference at the beginning of this letter
supplies just one of those graphic touches
which we so often miss in the usual historical
accounts. The office in question was that of
the *collectors*—a term which seems to have
lingered on till recently at Oxford. They were
candidates for B.A., appointed by the proctors
to distribute the other candidates into the
different schools, and to assign the order of
their disputations. In a sort of way they were
temporary pro-proctors. But the popular title
of "senior brother" is new to me, and I doubt
if any University historian had realized what
were the conventional demands made upon
them in the way of gifts and entertainments.

"Deer father I shall bee very glade to heare
from you by Mr. Rawlins when he comes by
Cambridge. I dayly expect his arrivall with
my sword by his side. I desire you to send
it by him when hee comes, for in the meane
time you have left mee altogether destitute of
a weapon. My tutor would have my armes

with the Colledge armes set upon my plate,
and if it please you I will send it up to you
to have it done: for there is not one at
Cambridge whiche can do it well. Basse (his
younger brother, Bassingborne) is admitted
and is very much in love with the university.
Wee remember our humble dutyes unto you
craving your blessing, and so I rest your
obedient sonne

WILLIAM GAUDY.

Doctor Welles is very sicke of a fever and
wee greatly feare that hee will never escape it.
May 1 1632."

(Addressed)   To my very loving father Mr.
Framlingham Gaudy Esquire in Fleet Street
at Mr. Wardes house a barber right over against
the kinges head tavern give these."

The reference to a sword is curious. It
shows—as do other similar references elsewhere—that the dictates of fashion soon prevailed over statute injunctions. The wearing
of a sword was stringently forbidden, for every
student, by Dr. Caius; but young men of
fashion evidently dressed here as they pleased,
and as they were accustomed to do elsewhere.
The plate which he mentions is of course the
customary gift made to the College by fellow-
commoners when they left. Mr. Gawdy's plate
seems to have disappeared long since. Robert
Wells, M.D., was a Fellow. He died the next
day, and left his estate and library to the
College.

" Sir I beseeche you let us expect our horses at Barton Milles (by Mildenhall, a stage on the Norwich road) upon the eleventh day of December being Wednesday: where we will meet them with our hackneys. I feare wee shall pay very deere for our Hackneys because the King will be at Newmarket about the same time. I pray send us word by this bearer whether you will send our horses to Barton upon the day prefixed: or whether you intend some other day. As for the paiment of tuition for my brothers, all schollers doe pay theire tutors as well absent as when they are in the Colledge. Wee remember our Humble dutyes to you and crave your blessing.

I rest your obedient sonne
WILL GAUDY.

(Caius Col.)
Nov. 19, 1633."

It is sometimes asked how the men got home from Cambridge, at a time before stage-coaches were introduced. The very poor probably stayed in College, or got a lift in the carrier's cart:—the days were now mostly past when they tramped it on foot.[1] The sons of country gentry, like William Gaudy and his brothers, as

---

[1] Similar shifts had to be adopted in much later days. The first time that my father brought me to Cambridge, as a boy, before the opening of the Railway, he drove us in his phaeton from London, sending his own horse on to Ware, and hiring one to take us thither. He used to tell me that in his day the difficulties for students who wanted to go North were considerable. The richer men posted, at any rate as far as Alconbury on the Great North Road. The poorer got a lift, as they could, so far; and then waited at the famous Inn there till some coach came by with a vacant seat on the top.

we see, had horses sent from home to take them the whole, or part of, the way. Harling is some 35 or 40 miles from Cambridge.

The next is from a younger brother of William. He entered in 1632, as "pensioner at the bachelors' table," a sort of intermediate position between the ordinary pensioner and the fellow-commoner.

"Deare father my dutie remembred unto you, and I did——receive your letter, and as for my box I had it at the carriers on Monday, the 22 of June, and after the reading I doe intende to cum downe, which will bee about seven weekes hence, for there will be almost none in the house, for they are allmost gone allready, and there will not be above 12 at the reading at the most, and after the reading the breake up commons, and I hope you will send me a peece for my money will not hold out; if you do not I must borrow it sumwhere, and so hoping you all are well, as I am, I rest your obedient sonne

BASSINGBOURNE GAUDY.

(Caius Col.)   July 4, 1635."

The "reading" referred to above may perhaps be that of the names of the graduates at "Commencement," the final ceremony of the year. If so, it lingered as a survival to very recent times, in the reading of the names in the *Ordo Senioritatis*, or Mathematical Tripos.

"Dear father I writ unto you the last weeke by our Cambridge carrier, but because I heard not from you againe, I suspect that my letter

cam not unto you. I directed it to Mr Neelsons
in Fleet Street at the signe of the talbot the
next doore to white friers gate : but now my
cousen Doll coming to Cambridge (where she
determines to continue) I understand by her
where your lodging is. I therefore hope that
this letter will bee safely convayed unto you. I
have bin of late very sicke of an ague, but nowe
(thankes bee to god) I am perfectly recovered,
only my physicke and my dyet in my sickness
being chargeable unto mee I hope you will consider mee for it at Easter or else this quarter
breakes mee. I writ unto you concerning my
hat which (if you buye a new one before Easter)
I desire you to bring down with you new
shagged and a new silver hatband of the best
fashion, for my old hat begins to be nought. I
pray you likewise to buy mee a silver girdle of
the best sort and bring it down with you and I
will pay for it againe. My cosen Doll arrived
yesternight at Cambridge with her man,
goodman Goblet, and intendes to sojourne at
ones house that was one of Anthony's mis-
tresses, but now married to a draper in Cambridge. I desire you to send for us, as soone as
ever you come to Harling : in the meane time
remembring our dutye unto you, craving your
blessing I rest

Your dutifull sonne

WILLIAM GAUDY.

(circa 1630)."

If, as is perhaps the case, the reference to his
cousin Anthony (of the former letters) is to be

taken in its most natural interpretation, it suggests a rather strange view of the state of things amongst the richer classes in College at that time. As to the attire, the statute bearing on the subject may be quoted: " . . . si pensionarius major (*i.e.* fellow - commoner), mulcta esto sex solidi et octo denarii, maxime si in publicum prodeat indecenter, hoc est sine veste longa et scholastica et pileo quadrato capiti apto."

"Deare Father, I am very glad to heare by my cosen Anthony that you enjoy your health. I have bin very much troubled with an ague, but nowe I thank god it hathe perfectly left mee. I understand by my cosen Anthony that you doe not knowe what my Tutor meaneth, in his last bill, by Cambridge commons: it is onely 3s. 8d. whiche wee pay every quarter for the deanes and other College officers wages, as well when we are absent as present. I would entreat you that my cosen Doll may make us a great Cake or twoe, and withall a cheese or twoe will doe very well to amend our poore lenten commons: whiche if you please to send you may by this carrier at his return backe again, who has promised mee to call for them as hee returnes to Cambridge. Hee is a very honest fellowe, and whatsoever you doe intend to send to us at any time, hee will safely deliver. So with my dutye remembred unto you, and craving your blessing, I rest

Your obedient sonne

WILLIAM GAUDY

(circa 1631)."

Here again we obtain a graphic little touch
as to the daily life. The general poverty of
College fare, especially at Lent, was of course
well known; but I do not remember to have
heard elsewhere that the students, like modern
—or former—schoolboys, had hampers sent from
home to help them out.

"Deare father, I am very sorry to understand, that you have gotten your ague againe.
I pray God (whoe hath perfectly restored mee to
my former health) deliver you out of your sick-
nesse. Cambridge is a very sickly place, for
there dy many every weeke of agues and other
diseases. I received the thinges you sent by
the carrier. I pray let Morris put my spare-
hawke into the mewe, for I hope shee will prove
a good one. Soe withe my duty remembred
unto you and craving your blessinge I rest

Your dutifull sonne

Gon. & Cai.   WILLIAM GAWDY.
    Marche the 10th (? 1632)."

"Deer father I am very glad to heare of your
amendment, I hope shortly to heare newes of
your perfect recovery. I have heere sent you
my plate with a pattern of the Colledge armes;
and likewise of my owne, because I would have
them placed in this order that you see uppon
the forefront of the plate. Within it I have put
the top of the eare whiche was broken off by
mischance. You see how miserably it is
battered broken and crackt, and withall howe
small it is: I therefore hope that you will
change it for a better. It will not bee muche

amisse considering how acceptable it will bee
to the Colledge, whoe doe expect a better piece of
plate from mee: I would not have it said
amongest them that mine is the worst in the
Colledge, which ollready it is. I hope that you
will not deny so reasonable a request. So
remembring our dutyes unto you, craving your
blessing I rest

Your obedient sonne

June 5 (? 1632)."   WILL. GAUDY.

"Sir I hope you will not taxe me of neglect
because as yet I have not writ unto you since I
was last at home. This is the firste carrier
whiche I could perswade to call at Harling,
whiche hee has faithfully promised mee to doe
at his returne from Norwich to Cambridge. I
pray send mee up the bible by him whoe will
bring it very safely: let Rawlins binde it up in
paper and binde two pieces of pastbord over it,
and it can take noe hurt. It has bin my hard
fortune to have had my old bible stolne (as I
suppose) out of my study in my absence: whiche
(thoughe I have made greate enquiry after) I
cannot heare of againe. It will bee no small
comfort to us to see you as you goe to London,
if you doe goe. In the meane time I expect your
letter, crave your blessing, and (my brothers
dutyes and mine remembred unto you) rest

Your obedient sonne

February 5, 1632-3   WILL. GAUDY.
(Caius Col.).

I pray sir bid Winter send mee my old frize
suite by this carrier."

The reference to his "study" may need a few words of explanation. As is well known, one room served for two or more students, even of the upper class, till a considerably later period than this. But for purposes of study, each of these chambers had two, or possibly three, very small rooms opening out of it. They were scarcely more than cupboards, and were sometimes made by boarding off a corner of the larger room. They were commonly known as "studies." Some of these rooms still survived in the disused attics of the Legge Buildings in the Tree Court, pulled down in 1868. A picture of one of these is given by Willis in the *Architectural History of Cambridge* (III. 308).

The writer of the next letters was a cousin of the last, but belongs to the following generation. He was a fellow-commoner at Christ's, where he entered in 1654. He took no degree. The tutor whom he praises so highly was Ralph Widdrington, afterwards Public Orator, and successively Professor of Greek and of Divinity. We gather, from Dr. Peile's College History, that Widdrington was a dexterous and pushing man who succeeded in retaining, during one stage of those troublous times, the offices which he had obtained during another. But the opinion as to his great popularity as a tutor is fully confirmed.

"Honoured Father

I cannot but acknowledge your care, and returne to you many thanks, for placing me under soe diligent a Tutor, and in so good society, but there are some things wanting which I must trouble you to furnish me with. I sent for the trunkes which were my uncle Ro. in which I thought to have found a paire of sheetes, but there were none. I want also half a douzen of napkins which are to be used in the hall which in the meantime I am con- strained to borrowe, and some small table clothes and towells and a piece of plate. So I rest having nothing else wherewith I may subscribe my self

Your most dutifull son

"Sir
BASS. GAUDY."

I received my hatte and an hat case, which I intend to keepe for to preserve my hatte. Sir, I desire you to send me twelve shillings for to cleare the cookes bill. I hope you will excuse me for being so short. So I rest

You most obedient son

BASSINGBOURNE GAUDY.

I pray bid my brother John send me some of his picters to dress up my study."

The reference to pictures for College rooms at that date seems to indicate a very exceptional state of things. In inventories and wills of this date such articles are quite unknown. But there certainly would not be much room to spare for them in a "study." "Napkins to be used in the hall" were of course a real necessary in the days before forks were invented. They are often referred to, and there were rules forbidding the use of tablecloth as a substitute.

" Sir

I have had a minde a long time to study mathematicks and shall be very glad to busy my selfe about it, if you please to be at the charge. It will be of some charge because I beleeve my Tutor is not skilled in it, and there is a man in towne who makes it his whole profession and hath teached very many. If you think it fitting, I would desire you to write to my Tutour to get this man to learne me, for it will be better taken from you than from me. I desire you to get Glover to make me a paire of sarcinate tops out of my mony. So I rest

Your most obedient son

BASS. GAUDY.

(Christ's Coll. circa 1655)."

It is a pity that we are not given the name of the Mr. Hopkins, or Dr. Routh, of the day, who made it " his whole profession " to teach mathematics. But the reference reminds us of the well-known fact that the specializing in this direction at Cambridge was a matter of later date than this.

" Sir

I have at last sent you a booke ruled with red lines, but with no clasps, the bookbinder says that it is better without. I go on in my french and have profitted so far as to make a piece of french. Sir I hope you will give me a stuffe suit, because you abated the vli; for 35 shillings was laid out for my saddle, neither did I use any extravagancy in laying

out the rest. A suit cannot come in better
time, for mine is very thredbare. I must have
a coat to it, to weare when I come to Bury.
Sir I would be glad to have my horse up if
you do not use him. You may allow that heir
which he stands you in there, for I suppose
you never use him after yr journey out of
Norfolke. The small Pox is reife in towne,
there dyed a fellowecommoner of Caius Colledge
last weeke. So I rest yr most obedient son
(? 1655)."   BASS. GAUDY.

The reference to learning French, repeated
in the next letter, is one of many indications
of the widely divergent pursuits adopted by
men of different status in College. Young
Gaudy was a fellow-commoner, and had probably no thought of taking a degree. The
scholars and Sizars would probably have had
no time for such ornamental accomplishments.
But it is worth noticing that a French teacher
could then be found in Cambridge.

"Sir I received yr letter, wherein you gave
me notice that I shall receive my quarteridge this
weeke: you bid me send you word how much
my Frenchman hath had, he hath had 21s. for
entrance and 10s. for a month's teaching. Yr
booke cost 4s. 6d. and my saddle cost 1£. 15s.:
if you please you may send this up with my
quarteridge, which is 3li. 10s. 6d. in all. So
I rest having nothing else wherewith I may
subscribe myselfe
                    Yr most obedient son
(circa 1655)."   BASS. GAUDY.

The fee for the Frenchman—a guinea down, and ten shillings a month—seems fairly high, when we remember the total amount of his cousin's half-yearly bills. Many scholarships at that day, were not worth more than forty shillings a year.

"Sir I pray bid Ed. Crosse to carry my fowle linnen to Mrs. Oigdons. It seems he hath been so negligent as to keepe it all this tyme at Mrs. Sharps. The fellowes and my Tutour disagree worse than they have done yet: the fellows and ye master did behave themselves very unjustly in a business concerning a fellow commoner of my Tutours, ye businesse was only thus: they and another fell out, and because my Tutours puple had ye better, he was admonished, and that other escaped free from any punishment. Sir I had occasion to write to my uncle Charles, and I sent for 2 bookes, viz. Josephus and Camb. (Camden's) britannia. I shall keepe them very safe till you shall require them againe. I pray bid Ed. Crosse carry my bowles to the carrier this weeks, and send him downe to Mary Butlers to make haste of my linnen. So I rest

Your most obedient son
Bass. Gaudy."

William Gaudy, the writer of the next, was one of the few who proceeded to a degree. His "keeping his acts in the schools" refers, of course, to the system of public discussions which corresponded to our modern examination system.

"Deer Father, I have heer sent you my
tutor's bill from Midsommer to Michaelmas.
Hee remembers his service unto you, and
desires you to send him some money by him
that bringeth up our horses. Wee are both
well, I thanck God, enjoying our healthes as
well as if we were at Harling. I pray let us
heare from you by this bearer: my brother
Fram wanted money, and I make no question
but a crowne would come very seasonably to
supply his wante. So with our dutyes remembered unto you, craving your blessing I rest
Your dutifull sonne
WILLIAM GAUDY.
Upon Friday next I am to keep my actes in
the schooles.

November xxii, 1631."

"Deer father, I am very sorry to heare that
you have not your health at London: but I
trust in God that the next weeke I shall heare
from you that you are perfectly recovered. I
most humbly thank you for my sword, which I
received by Mr. Rawlins: it is a very good one,
and suche a one as I desired to have. Doctor
Wells (one of the senior fellows of the College)
is dead, and hath given all his estate to the
Colledge. My brothers and I (thanckes bee to
God) are in as good healthe as wee wishe unto
you: we remember our humble dutyes unto
you and crave your blessing. So I humbly take
my leave of you, and rest your dutifull sonne
WILLIAM GAUDY.
May 15, 1632."

The piece of plate referred to in the next is, of course, the customary presentation by every fellow-commoner on his leaving College. Unfortunately, like so very many other pieces of plate, this particular piece seems to have been lost or sold.

"May 22, 1632.

Dear father, I am very glad to heare by Mr. Barry of your perfect recovery. I beseech God to continue your health. I am dayly importuned by the Colledge to set my armes upon the plate with the colledge armes. If it please you to send mee word this weeke, I will send it to you to London with the pattern of the colledge armes: it is likewise very much battered and bruised and I have a great desire it should be mended before I present it to our master. If you thinke it fitting when you have it with you, you may change it for a better: for I have received many favours from the Colledge, which deserve to bee recompensed with a better piece of plate. I will leave to your discretion, because you knowe what is fittingest to be done. So with my humble duty unto you I rest

Your dutifull sonne
WILLIAM GAUDY."

Charles, the writer of the next, was a younger brother of William, whom he followed to Caius. The reference to a "chamber" persumably applies to a room of his own: till securing this he probably had to "chum" with one or more other students.

"Most loving father, my duty remembred unto you, sir, is to desire you for to send me up some linnin, two or thre paire of sheets and two or thre pillowbeares, and a tablecloth, and hauf a douson napkins, and two or thre towells, and sire as for my bedding you need not to sende it up untill I have a chamber, and when I have a chamber I will write you worde, and my tutor will get me one as soone as he can, and for these things that I writ unto you sire I will pray you to send them up by this bearere thereof and hoping you will be mindful of me for them and so I rest

Youer loving sone
CHARLES GAUDY."

Apparently, by the following letter, he soon had a chamber provided for him. What was the nature of the usual arrangements, it is difficult to say:—trifling domestic customs, which are too familiar to every one at the time to be worth describing, are often those which give most trouble to the later enquirer. Perhaps the bed and bedding had to be provided by the new occupant of a room, whereas those who shared a room with others found this ready provided.

"November 1, 1637.

Most loving father, my duty remembred unto you and I have received your letter and my linin that you sent me and nowe I have a chamber I will pray you to send me my beddinge up by the Cambridge wagon that comes to Thetford, and I will pray you to send

it to Thetford on Satterday and leve it at the
signe of the grayhound for the carire to call for
it that come a Monday, and I will pray you to
send me up some money for I have bene here a
great while without any; I will pray you to
send me some as soone as you can and so I rest

Youer dutifull sonne

CHARLES GAUDY."

The writer of the next, Bassingbourne, was a
brother of Charles and William. The reference
to pictures is curious, as current accounts of
the habits of students of those times would not
suggest the possession of such luxuries.

"Honoured father, I am sorry I have put you
to so much expense, and have so little regarded
both mine owne creditte and your condition:
the occasion of it was at my first coming to
Cambridge, most of it being laid out upon
necessaryes; but craving your pardon I shall
behave my selfe with such discretion and
thriftinesse as that you shall not feare to be
troubled any more in this kind, but shall receive
a faire testimony both of my good husbandry
and my endeavours to satisfye you in my
studyes; who is and ever will be

Your most obedient son

BASSINGBOURNE GAUDY.

I pray hasten my plate, for I stand in great
need of it. I pray remember my love to my
Brothers and bid my brother John to send me
some of his pictours."

LETTERS OF THE 17TH CENTURY 219

The reference to the "commencement" hardly needs explanation. It occurred in July, and was the equivalent, as a public ceremony, of the modern Degree Day.

"Honoured Father
I received my suit the last weeke, for which I returne you many thankes. I heard by Ro. Green that you had a hatte which was too little four you, which if you please to give it me I will be a very good husband in wearing it, for I have but one, and I weare that every day. I hope I shall see you heer at the commencement : it will be the publickest as have been these four yeares, so I rest having nothing else werewith I may subscribe myselfe
Your most obedient son
Bass. Gaudy."

"Sir, I had presented my duty sooner to you if an opportunity had bin presented sooner to mee, this being the first messenger I could lighte upon since my last arrivall at the university. Although it bee somewhat too soone to speake of our journey home yet (because it may soe happen that I may not lighte of another messenger between this and Christmas) I would desire you to send us word by this bearer what day we shall meet your horses at Barton Mills, or what other meanes you intend for our coming home. I beseeche you, Sir, remember your promise concerning my spare hawke. We are all well, I thanke God, and we hope the like of you. Furthermore,

remembring our duties, wee crave your blessinge. I rest

Your obedient sonne

WILL. GAUDY.

My brother Fram. has sent my tutors bill
enclosed.

November 8th."

Whether the "spare hawke" was intended for
use at Cambridge, in defiance of Dr. Caius'
statute, is not clear. If it were there can be no
doubt of the splendid opportunities for the
sport of hawking afforded by the wide extent of
waste land in the neighbourhood. Barton Mills,
near Mildenhall, it may be remarked, was mid-
way on the journey home. Evidently the
common practice was adopted of having the
family horses sent to meet them there, whilst
the students themselves hired a mount from
Cambridge.

"Dear father,   heare that Franke Gaudy
comes downe by the waggon: if it be so
(although your trunke comes not downe before
Easter) yet hee may bring my hat downe with
him very conveniently: the cause why I thus
hasten you is because my old hat will not bee
agreeable to my newe clothes which I shall
nowe buy at Easter, and I knowe not into what
company I shall happen when I am in the
countrey. I have taken order that our horses
may meet us at Cambridge that night that you
come hether, that we may go downe with you.
The king defers his coming to Cambridge until

the 19th of this month, and it is a question
whether he will come or no: so with our dutyes
remembred unto you, craving your blessing I
rest

Your obedient sonne

WILL. GAUDY."

King Charles I, and his queen, did come a
fortnight afterwards, so we may hope that the
new hat was in time :—if indeed he was allowed
to put it on during such a ceremonial academic
occasion. The customary festivities were held,
and many honorary degrees were conferred, on
the occasion of this royal visit,—the first held
by this king.

"Sir, I wrot to you the other day, but
because my messenger proved unfaithfull I
could not have them thinges sent unto me
which I expected at his returne. I have taken
my old messenger into my favoure againe,
and hee has promised to make mee amendes
for his former delinquency. I pray send mee
the bible by him safely packed up by Mr.
Rawlins: you heard in my last letter what
hard fortune I had in the losse of my other.
We doe expect something from you this lent to
helpe our poore commons; I hope my cousen
Doll will looke to provide us somethinge.
Easter drawes neere nowe and I hope wee
shall see you shorteley. Meanewhile wee remember our dutyes unto you and I rest

Your obedient sonne

WILL. GAUDY."

The hint given in the above letter, that, whereas the practice of fasting in Lent was (statutably) kept up so far as the College table was concerned, the consequent rigour was mitigated by the conveyance of hampers from home, is amusing. It is just one of those little touches which we only obtain from private letters. Readers of the former letters may remember that "cousen Doll" had been appealed to on a previous occasion to make and send them "a great cake or two," and to supplement the supply with "a cheese or two," with the same object of helping out "the poor lenten commons." We should not have supposed that this resource was necessary, for, from a report sent to Archbishop Laud only four years after the above letter must have been written, we are told that "Upon Frydays and all Fastingdays, the victualling houses prepare Flesh, good store, for all scholars . . . upon all such fasting nights in schollers chambers are generally the best suppers of the whole week, and for the most part of Flesh meate all." Perhaps the young Gawdys found it nicer and cheaper to send home for what they wanted.

"Sir, I received your letter by Tho. Ship and the other papers, and amongst them my Tutour's last bill, which truly at the first sight did amaze me as well as your selfe, but after that I had considered everything I began to fear that it was right, for this bill is an halfe year bill, that which was behind hand was the bill from Midsommer to Michaelmas; he hath had

but £7 for all this halfe year: my Tutour hath
sent you the bill at large in his letter. The
day after I came to towne (Cambridge) I and
Mr. Anderson, who presents his services to you,
and Tho. Ship went to buy my gowne, which
comes to 7li. 12s. 6d., and the making 15s. I
hav paid it. Sir you writte to me to forbear
silver buttons, but bothe my Tutor and Mr.
Anderson did perswade me to it: it did cost
but 20s. the more: if you think it too much I
will abate it in my allowance. I have sent you
mine hatcase, that you may send up my new
hat: I have very much need on it: if you stand
in need of money for the present I can stay for
it this month. I pray send me word how my
Grandfather doth. So I rest

Your most obedient son

BASS. GAUDY."

If the price for the gown referred to above
seems very high, regard had to the then value
of money, it must be remembered that young
Gaudy was a fellow-commoner. Did the silver
buttons correspond to the silver lace of modern
times?

"Sir, I have sent you two bookes, viz.
Martialls Epigrams and Goodwins antiquities,
and what booke you intend to have next I
pray you send me word wher you please to
have it. My Tutour remembers his service to
you, and desires to be excused by reason he
doth not writte to you: the reason is he is sicke
with a quartin ague, and hath been so this
month. I pray send me the leather wesket

you promised me by the carryer. I pray send
my Tutour up some money as soon as you can:
so I rest

Your most obedient son

BASSINGBOURNE GAUDY."

"Sir I received my 50s. and the other mony
for my Tutour: you bid me take the mony
which I laid out for my gowne out of my
Tutours, but it will be as well if I stay the
longer and have it from you, Shipps bill for
my gowne comes to 10s. 6d.: my quarter day
was out last sonday, for although I have not
been here a full quarter yet I must pay for
tuteridge and detriments and Barber and such
things as well as if I had been heer the whole
quarter. I pray pay Mrs. Pidgeon this quarter
out of my mony, so I shall expect mony to
begin a new quarter and that which is behind
all which I beleeve I owe my Tutour for my
commons and tuteridge and other things, I
have sent you two wisks, but I can get no
paper all over the towne. I would be very
glad to hear how things are ordered in Norfolke,
where my uncles live and my brother Fra.
The paper which you sent me signifyed nothing
but my income which I received under my
Tutours hand, in which he was mistaken, for
it seems my income comes to 12li. 10s. besides
my chayres. I make no question but that I
shall live very well upon 60li. per annum. So
I rest

Your most obedient son

BASS. GAUDY."

" Sir After that I had writte my other letter I forgotte one thing which is that you must either make me a blacke taffety wascoat, or else halfe shirts; I would wish you to buy me a black cloacke to weare with my suit when I come into the country; there will be nothing lost by it, for when I have done mourning it will make me a suit. So I rest

Your most obedient son
BASS. GAUDY."

"Worthy Sir I am deeply ingaged to a prockter in Cambridge a dear friende of myne to doe him so much favour as to give him a Bucke this commensment, and having noe other meanes but yourself to effect yt I desir you would doe me the curtesie to make good that I have promysed: your faithful Brother and Servant

CHARLES GAUDY."

There was, as is well known, much feasting and mutual entertainment especially at Commencement time. Charles Gaudy did not himself take any degree, but presumably he felt himself bound, as a man of family, to see that his friend carried out his entertainment in due style.

The writer of the next was a fellow-commoner, which accounts for his having a sizar to wait upon him. These private, or "proper" sizars (the term lingered till lately, if indeed now extinct, at Trinity), were in those days to all intents valets. They waited on their

Q

masters, and with their payment and free board managed to support themselves till they graduated.

" Deere mother. I have received your kind tokens by my cousen Gayor, and the pies which you sent me, and my cosen Charlie, by the carrier: for which thinges and for many other kind remembrances my thankes are beyond expression. As for a sizer, about which you writt unto mee, I am already provided. I hope to see you with my fathers permission at Harling this Easter, but in the meane time money is very scarce with me, which want I hope you will soone supply. So, my humble duty being remembred unto you, I rest

Your dutifull and obedient sonne

WILLIAM GAUDY.

Gon. & Cai. Coll.

March 3 (1630?)

I pray remember me to Mr. Rawlins, and tell him that I would pray him to send mee my watche as soone as he can conveniently."

" Deare father, I have suche an urgent cause that I cannot forbeare from writing unto you these few lines, wherein I humbly entreat you to supply my wants, whiche if you do not my credite is in daunger. There are many in our Colledge who doo thinke that I am so miserable that I will not parte withe my money, and oftentimes doo deride mee for it: which faulte (you knowe) lies not in my power to mend unless I had wherwithal to shewe myself more free and liberall. It is not the covetousnesse

of my minde whiche makes me thus, but only
the want and scarsity of money. Every one doe
expecte of mee, being a fellowe commoner, that
I should live after the fashion of a gentleman,
whiche by no means in the world I can accom-
plishe without the helpe of money. I knowe it
is your desire that I should live conformable
to my callinge, whiche if you would have mee to
do I beseech you (if you tender my credite) to
send mee your kind answer with some money
enclosed in it by this bearer. So with my duty
remembred unto you, in haste I rest and will
ever remaine

Your dutyfull and obedient sonne

WILLIAM GAUDY."

" Dear father, we arrived at last at Cambridge, though not without muche annoyance of
winde and raine : it rained all the way wee rid
from Newmarket to Cambridge. My tutor is
not now in the Colledge, nor yet Rob. Eade, but
we looke for them very shortly. I hope that if
you goe to London wee shall see you as you
passe by : if not then yet at Christmas wee shall
visite you. In the mean time we shall remaine
your dutifull sonnes, studying (as much as in us
lyeth) to continue in your fatherly love and good
opinion of us. My conscience telleth mee that
as yet I have committed nothing worthy of your
displeasure and by God's assistance I hope it will
long so continue, partly in respect of my owne
good but principally to give you contentment
and satisfaction ; for I desire to have my being
no longer than I continue in your love and

favour. So with ower duties remembred unto you and craving your blessing, I rest
Your ever dutyfull and obedient sonne
WILLIAM GAUDY."

(Caius College,
Circa 1637-8.)

"Most loving Father (my duty remembered unto you) I dide receive your letter that you sent me in my tutours letter a fortnete agoe: I would a' write then but that I could not conveniently write unto you; and the cause of my writing now Sir, is to praye you to send me some money, for I have been here allmost a yeare, and you have sent me none, therefore the next time the carrier com this way I would pray you to send me some though it be but a little; and as for my bedding I pray you send it up when you please; and so I rest
your dutyfull sonne
CHARLES GAWDY.

To his loving father Mr Framlingham Gaudy Esquire at West Harling, give these. Leve this letter at Mr Sneelnes the Tanneries to be sent us."

As regards the application for money in these letters, it must be remembered that the tutor supplied, or paid for, every thing that could be considered an ordinary requirement for a student, books, even clothes as a rule, being thus settled for with parent or guardian. There were no college clubs, and very few opportunities of spending money in ways not forbidden by academic statutes. For the poorer students a very small sum, possibly only a few shillings a term, would be really needed for them to pay out of pocket.

(Caius College,
1637-8.)

"Most loving Father my duty remembred unto you, and my tutour have sent a bill of that quarter when I was in the countrie, and he would pray you to send 5 poundes by the carrier when he come up againe to pay for my commons this quarter: and as for the sickness ther have died more the last fortnet nor this: And so I rest

Your dutyfull sonne
CHARLES GAWDY."

The reference to "that quarter when I was in the countrie" applies doubtless to the Long Vacation, when as a rule only scholars and sizars were in residence. The "sickness" mentioned is presumably the plague, of which there had been a very bad outbreak a year or two .before, and which was probably still lingering in the town. In all the severer visitations of the kind the students were as far as possible dismissed; the very poor, and those who had no home to go to, being allowed to remain within the carefully locked College gates.

(Caius College
1637-7.)

"Most loving Father, my duty remembred unto you, and I dide receive youer letter, and

I will pray you for to appointe some body to get
my thinges ready, that I did write unto you
before, for I have appointed a carier to bringe
them up, and when he come this way againe
he will call for them : and a chamber I have
not yet and I shall have one as soone as our
master or my tutour can get me one, and
when I have one I will write you word for
my bedding, and so I rest

your dutifull sone

CHARLES GAUDY."

The reference to a " chamber " above, is not
quite clear. The ordinary students, as is well
known, in Elizabethan days were crowded
three or four together in one room, which
they shared with their tutor. By 1637, the
date in question, more rooms had been built,
and there was probably less crowding. But only
a fellow-commoner (and Charles Gaudy was not
one) could have had a room to himself. What
he was probably looking forward to was the
comparative luxury of sharing a chamber with
one companion.

" Sir my bound deutie unto you remembred
with hope of your good health, the continuance
thereof I doo desire to the Lords good will
and pleasure both now and ever : thankes be
to God my brothers at Cambridge be in good
health, and my brother Tho. at Bury and my
brother Rob. here remember his dutie to you.
I pray you good father send me a bible as
soone as you please, for I have great wante of

one to use at church and thus with my humble
dutie unto you good father remembred I rest
your dutifull and obedient sonne
CHARLES GAUDY.
Thetford, June 5, 1632."

The above, if correctly dated, must have
been written when returning from a visit to
his brothers, who were then at Cambridge,
before his own entry at College.

"Deer father, I desire to let no opportunity
slippe out of my handes, wherein I may present
oure dutyes unto you and certify you of our
wellfare. I am recovered (I thancke God) in
some sorte from the reliques of my ague; and
finde myselfe to growe stronger and in better
plighte. My brother Fram. likewise is very
well. My tutor nor Robert Eade (fellow of the
College) are not yet come to the Colledge, but
wee expect them every day. I pray let us heare
from you by the next messenger that passeth
this way, for you would not thinke what joy
and delighte your letters doe infuse into us.
But above all if you goe to London our joy
will exceed to see you at Cambridge. Thus
with our dutyes remembred unto you, craving
your blessing I rest
Your dutifull sonne
WILLIAM GAUDY.
Gon. & Cai. Coll.
October 24 1631."

"Dear father in your last letter your will
was that I should send you word in what time

it was fittest wee should come home. I desire
you (if you can conveniently) to send up our
horses upon Wednesday next being the 7th
day of this month; and I pray let not a horse
for my cosen Anthony be forgotten, who
remembers his humble service unto you. The
reason I would come home soone is, because
I cannot tell how soone after Christmas my
occasions concerning my commencement will
hasten my returne. So with our dutyes in
most humble manner remembred unto you,
craving your blessing and desiring you not to
faile at the time prefixed, I rest

your dutifull sonne
WILLIAM GAUDY.

December 2, 1631."

"Deer father this is the third letter which
I have written unto you since you last went to
London, but because I have not as yet heard
from you I conjecture that my other twoe have
been miscarried. I writ unto you the last weeke
concerning my plate, I would have my armes
engraven on it; which (because it cannot be
done at Cambridge) if it please you to send
mee word the next week I will send it to you
to have it done at London. Besides it is very
much battered and broken and I would faine
have it mended. If you think it fitting you may
change it for a better. Wee are very well (I
thank God) only my brother Fram. is very
poore, and most humbly beseeches you to
supply his wantes with us. You should comfort
us very muche to heare from you, though it

were expressed but in towe or three lines. So
with our dutyes remembred I rest
Your dutifull sonne
WILL GAUDY.
May 29, 1632.

To my very loving father Mr. Framlingham
Gaudy Esquire at Mr Wardes house, a barber in
Fleet Street right over against the King's head
tavern."

" Deere father I am not a little glad to heare
of the perfect welfare of you and all our household, considering the distress into whiche you
were brought when I last left you. I hope that,
when I come home next, nothing will fall oute
so unfortunately as to procure our banishment
from your house, as it happened when wee were
last in the country. Within this fortnighte, or
three weekes at the farthest (according to your
promise when we cum away) wee shall expect
our horses : I heare by the carrier that our newe
orchard goes forward with greate expedition. I
have a longing desire to see it, which desire I
hope will be shortly accomplished. I have heer
sent a booke with this letter, whiche is newly
come out and I thincke it is worthe the reading,
if it please you to take the paynes to puruse it.
So with my humble duty remembred unto
you craving your fatherly blessing I rest
Your obedient sonne
WILL GAUDY.
My brother Bass. remembers his humble
duty to you.
Novem. 19, 1632."

"Truly Sir, amongst all the commodities which I enjoy heer at Cambridge, I find nothing prejudiciall to mee, but onely that I am so remote from my friends whiche if it pleaseth you you may supply by giving mee leave to come and visite you this vacation, which thinge I doe not request of you for the cause of absenting myself from my studies, but onely for the desire whiche I have to see you and my deare mother. I would therefore entreate you having already obtained leave of my tutor to come and see you within this fortnight or three weeks, that you would about that time send me an easy going horse, whereby the journey may be the lesse troublesom unto me. So with my humble duty remembred unto you and expecting one of your men with a horse at the prefixed time, I rest

Your dutifull and obedient sonne

WILLIAM GAUDY."

"Deare father I hope you will pardon my negligence in that you have not received any letters from me since my last coming to Cambridge, the cause whereof proceedeth from diverse businesses wherewith I have bin employed since I have taken possession of my newe chambers. Truly I am very much beholden to our maister for that hee hath bestowed them upon mee, for they are as convenient chambers as any are in all the colledge, which Mr. Rawlings can testify unto you. I have heare sent you my tuitours bill, which at the first view will seem to be very large, but when you

see the incom of my chamber and my fireing
this winter, and other necessaries in it, the
which you shall never find in my bill againe,
your mind will bee soone altered from your
former cogitations. I hope you will not be
unmindfull of my late requests unto you to
send me another suit of apparrell which I make
no doubt but you will yield unto, consideringe
what need I shall have when I come home at
Christmas. I pray let mee receive your answer
by this bearer with som kind token enclosed in
it. So my duty being remembred unto you I
rest

> your dutyfull and obedient sonne
>> WILLIAM GAUDY."

"Dear mother, in the last letter which I
received from you by the carrier you promised
mee that you would send mee the cakes and
cheeses. I therefore hope to receive them from
you upon Saturday by this carrier, who is a
very honest fellowe, and hathe promised mee to
call in our house alwaies, when hee cometh into
Norfolke which is once a fortnighte, and will
bring up letter or anything for me which you
will send. I would entreate you to make me
some boothose tops and send me against Easter.
So with my humble duty remembred unto you
and my good father, and expecting your answer,

> I rest your dutyfull and obedient sonne
>> WILLIAM GAUDY.

Cambridge March 8.

When you send me a letter backe againe you
should doe very well to put an angel or halfe a
piece into it."

"Deer mother, I hope you will not bee unmindfull of the promises which you made unto mee the last Christmas the time being now com wherein they shoulde bee fullfilled; but as for them things I will leave them to your own discretion to send them when you think fittinge. My man is now a going away from mee to London to dwell there, but I am very glad to thincke that I have given him no occasion of his departure; the cause of his departure being the desire (which I thincke most men have) to live in London. So with my duty remembred unto you and my good father, craving both your blessings, I rest

your ever dutifull and obedient sonn

WILLIAM GAUDY.

"Deare mother, I heartily thancke you for your kind tokens. My tutor likewise (remembring his service unto you) is very thankfull unto you. Nowe concerning the things for whiche I writ unto you for truly I received them from my cosen Gayor but they were very much too big for mee, wherefore I have heer sent them unto you, entreating you to send to my cosen Gayor, to change them and send mee another paire of the same colour by the carrier. So my humble duty remembred unto you and to my good father, in haste I rest

your dutifull and obedient sonne

WILLIAM GAUDY.

From Gon. & Cai. Coll.
Novem. 5, 1629."

It is worth remarking that there is no reference in the above letter to a matter on which the bulk of his fellow-students were probably taking a keen interest. The fifth of November was one of the days for the college bonfire:—the authorities at that time encouraged these displays rather than the reverse. In fact the bursar generally entered the charge in the college accounts.

It may be added that William, the writer of the above letters, was the eldest son, and entered as a fellow-commoner. He was one of the very few in that position who proceeded to a degree. He afterwards entered at the Inner Temple, and in due time succeeded his father at West Harling. He was created a baronet in 1663.

" Sir, I writte to you the last weeke to desire you to send me some mony for the cookes bill, which comes to 12s, but fearing that my letter should have misscarryed I presume to trouble you again, desiring you to send it me. I pray send me those saltsellers which you promised me when you were at Cambridge. I stand in very much want of plate. So remembring my love to my brothers, I rest

Your most obedient son,

BASS. GAUDY.

To his much honoured Father William Gaudy Esq. at Mrs Sharpe's house in Bury St. Edmunds."

Bassingbourne, the writer of the above and of the next two letters, was a son of William above. He was at Christ's College, where he entered as a fellow-commoner in 1654. He resided for about two years and a half, but did not proceed to a degree.

It may be mentioned, as an illustration of the almost entire absence of what would now be called the democratic spirit in the English Revolution, as compared with the French, that the institution of fellow-commoners was in no way interfered with. They remained about as numerous as before, and retained all their old rank and privileges.

" Sir, you must needs furnish me with some money this weeke by the carrier. He will be very trusty to deliver it to me. My tutour gave up his quarter bills this weeke to his pupills, and my bill which I must pay him this weeke. If you have not payd Mrs Pidgeon for the last quarter I pray do it. I shall expect an answer of this letter and of the last this weeke. So I reste

your obedient son

Bass. Gaudy."

" Sir you told me that you would have me come into the country this Whitsontide. If it be your pleasure I may have a very good opportunity to come home with Mr Pigeon, who will be here this week with Mr Poley fellow-commoner. I shall be very well furnished with an horse, for Thomas Glover offers to lend me his horse all the time that I am in the country. Sir, if it be your intention that I

should come, I desire you to send me word
tomorrow, which you may do if you please but
to wright a letter and send it this night to Mr
Browne the Wollen Draper who comes to Newmarket, and will deliver it to one that will
deliver it to mee, the reason because I would
know so speedily is because I would send my
things by the carryer to be ready against I
come. So I rest

your most obedient son

Bass. Gaudy.

To his very loving friend (i.e. father), William
Gaudy, Esq. at Mrs Sharpe's house in Bury."

It will be noticed that the above letters to
William Gaudy are addressed, not to W.
Harling but to lodgings at Bury. This, combined with the fact that he obtained a baronetcy
soon after the Restoration, raises a presumption
that he was a Royalist whose estates had been
sequestrated.

XII.

LETTERS OF AN 18TH CENTURY STUDENT.

The following letters I owe to the kindness of the late Mr. Albert Hartshorne, of Charlton, Shepton Mallet, who sent me transcripts from his own large collection of family papers. The letters were addressed to Mr. Hartshorne's maternal grandfather, Thomas Kerrich, well known in Cambridge as the University Librarian, and as a man of much artistic knowledge and skill. The writer was Framingham Willis, son of Thomas Willis, of Brancaster, Norfolk. He was admitted pensioner of Caius College, June 25, 1767. He was afterwards a Fellow of the College from 1772 to 1776, and was presumably by profession a barrister, as he entered at the Middle Temple. He changed his name to Thurston in after life.

The picture of College life thus presented is in several ways of much interest. The date corresponds with almost the lowest period of the fortunes of the University during the last 350 years. The total numbers had then shrunk sadly since the brilliant days before the Civil Wars; and, with the fall of numbers, discipline had relaxed, and teaching, both Collegiate and University, had almost disappeared. I have described the state of things in the *Biographical History;* but these letters give evidence of a fact to which I have also called attention, viz.

that at this time of depression there were never wanting students who in their own quiet way,— with few examinations to help, or hinder, them, and no prizes to reward,—took a real interest in their work.

1.

" Dear Sir,

Since I had the happiness to see you last I have been admitted of this college, where I am now resident. From the observations I have been able to make, I must be of opinion that a College life, for one of a serious turn, and contemplative disposition, is the most delightful situation imaginable. My residence here, however, was at first, a little uncomfortable, where I could hardly see a single person whom I had met with before, or anyone who might instruct me in the ways and customs of the place. But this awkwardness is worn off now, and I am almost as perfectly settled in College as one who has led the greater part of his life in it. Since my being here I have taken a view of all the Colleges, which has been I think the pleasantest time I ever spent in my life. You would hardly believe it is in the power of art to furnish out such a multitude of noble buildings as you here meet with. Here is every convenience allotted to the Students that can possibly be expected from the benefactions of kings and queens. I do not believe, as good a painter as you are, that you can fancy finer walks than those about Trinity College,

R

or a more magnificent edifice than the College itself. I am, however, so singular as to prefer Clare Hall to any of the rest. It is neat beyond description; and though it might not at first sight strike your fancy so much as Trinity, yet the more you consider, the more you admire it; whereas the surprize occasioned by a magnificent appearance wears off, after once or twice seeing, and the beauty of it is lost insensibly. I have to-day seen the public Library where the Learning of all ages is represented, and to which something is added every day. The number of books in it is supposed to be upwards of seventy thousand.

Can you, my dear Sir, or rather can you not yet discern, to what all this prattle tends? Can you conceive, why I should lavish uselessly ink and paper, to describe to you things with which you will presently be well acquainted? In few words it is no more than this. I most heartily wish for your company here; and as you have no longer any apprehensions of the small pox, I see nothing to hinder it. It was once I know your father's intention to have you reside here before the commencement, and by that means to escape the odious title of a Term Jobber. I wish heartily that he may continue in that resolution; and be assured you may depend on any assistance that lies in my power at your first setting out; and perhaps I may be well enough acquainted with the College custom to give help to one who is a perfect stranger.

I congratulate you and your sister on your

recovery from the small pox; to whom as well
as to your father, pray present my compliments.

I am, Dear Sir,
Your most assured friend,
and obedient servant,
FRAM. WILLIS.

Caius College,
June 30th, 1767."

2

" Dear Sir.

Your not coming up to College as soon as
you expected, I assure you, is a cutting disappointment to me. I had laid my account
with having a friend resident here, during the
whole vacation, with whom I might in agreeable
converse pass away the minutes, which every
one must allow for a recreation from study.
Such a disappointment is the more severely
felt at this time, as the University is always very
thin during the long vacation; and there will
not, in a week's time be one Undergraduate
left in Caius besides myself. The objection you
make to coming up immediately, I must beg
leave to say, is very frivolous. Your being
already admitted will prevent the examination
you so much dread: and let me tell you the
examination at a person's first being admitted,
though it were much more strict than it
generally is, is very easily passed through,
and hardly deserves to be stiled any thing
else than a mere matter of form. My Tutor,

when I first went to him, only desired me to construe an ode in Horace, a few lines in the beginning of a Satire in Juvenal, not more than three sentences in one of Cicero's Orations, and as many verses out of the Greek Testament. A Homer indeed was produced; but as it had a Latin version quite uncovered, which, if there had been occasion, I might with one single glance of my eye have had recourse to, it hardly deserves to be mentioned. The examination by the Master and Dean was still more easy than the Tutor's.

If this be only an objection started by yourself, if the fear of an examination deters you from getting settled here, I hope I have by this time removed it: and if your father has no more weighty reasons to alledge against your coming up immediately, I shall still expect the pleasure of your Company.

Your opinion that Magdalen is the worst College in the University seems founded upon prejudice, rather than on reasonable ground. The College is but badly situated, and, I think, not overstocked with Undergraduates, but it has one ornament, by which it outshines not only all the Colleges here, but perhaps all the Universities in the world—the best mathematician[1] and most able astronomer of them all. The Library there I have not seen. I apprehend it will be an easy matter for you to avail yourself of any advantage, which might be open to you from it, if you had liberty

---

[1] Edward Waring, Lucasian Professor in Mathematics.

to go and come as you please; for as long as
I have been in Cambridge I have not once got
admission into our library.

Your hint about not contracting too much
acquaintance at my first setting out, I am
obliged to you for. It was indeed what I had
determined against before my coming up.

I am, with compliments as before, Dear Sir,
Your most assured friend
and humble servant
FRAM. WILLIS.
Caius College.
July 18th, 1767."

3.

"Dear Sir.

Your last letter, bearing date the 3rd of
August, I did not receive till the 13th of this
month. Sure Cooper's people must have been
strangely negligent in not putting it into the
post office according to your direction. Your
questions are so very numerous that I am afraid
I shall not be able to answer them all in this
epistle, for want of room : but to begin with the
first. I must take the liberty to say, that your
asking me what purpose my residence here
during the vacation will answer, is absurd
enough. Pray what end do you think your
residence here in term-time will answer? you
will tell me that you come with a design to
study. I stay here for just the same reason,
and by the bye, I think this time the most
convenient for application. For though I like

books indifferently yet I love to enjoy my friends, which it is most convenient to do in term time, and there is an inconvenience you will be subject to at your first outset which you ought to guard against; that is the interruption of Loungers. There are but few people of this stamp in the university now; they are all gone down into the country, and none are left behind but those that are studiously inclined. Therefore this is an evil I am free from; and indeed I got a room up two pairs of stairs in order the more to have it in my power to dip (?) the *non domi* upon them. They are a set of people whom I much dislike; for they relish no scheme of diversion that you can propose to them, but take a pleasure in ruining two hours in a morning by idle chit-chat which may be applied to good advantage. You desire to know the manner I spend my time in College; but before I do this, I must tell you that you will be here your own master, and may do just what you please (so it be nothing wicked) without controul.

As I can do anything I please at this time especially, I spend a part of my time in a manner very different from what the rest of my acquaintance here do, in a manner which perhaps you may call whimsical. I generally rise at five, and then read for an hour; at six I take a pretty long walk, but so as to be back to chapel at seven. After chapel is done, three times a week I go to the cold bath,[1] and after that I come home to breakfast, which I take

---

1 There was then a bathing place in the Fellows' garden, like those still existing at Christ's and Emmanuel.

care to have over before nine. Then I sit down
to read for three hours and a half, and at half-
an hour after twelve my hair-dresser comes to
me, and I begin to dress for commons. You
will be obliged to comply with the custom of
putting on a clean shirt every day and of
having your hair dressed. After commons, if
ever, 'tis allowable to lounge away an hour at a
friend's room and drink a glass of wine, but this
is what I seldom do. At five I sometimes go to
a Coffee-house, where you meet with all the new
pamphlets, magazines, newspapers, &c., and
drink a dish of tea, coffee or chocolate. At six I
return to chapel, and after that I take a walk
on the walks if it be fine weather, if not, in
some college cloisters. At eight, your bedmaker comes to ask what you please to have for
supper, and gives you a bill of fare, which they
call here a size bill. They have always very
good things, but they are exorbitantly dear, as
you may guess by 3d for a common tart.
Persuade your father to let you have a good
allowance; if you keep whole terms, an hundred
pounds a year will not be sufficient. You will
be glad to hear that the custom of drinking is
entirely exploded in polite company; but I
would advise you never to seem afraid of drinking, for the bucks here will imagine by that,
that they can make you drunk very easily; and
to make a freshman drunk is excellent fun to
them. Your Tutor or your Master will probably
ask you to sup with them; if they do not I shall
be glad to see you with me the night of your
admission and then you will be in no danger to

be led into any excess. Does not your father come up with you?

An old acquaintance ought not to be dropped abruptly; always be civil and complaisant to him, but never go to his room to sup or engage in any scheme with him. He is very expensive I am told, and the character that he bears in the University is that of a d——d polite fellow, one who is a blood in all respects, but that he cannot afford to spend so much money.

Make yourself master of all common arithmetick and decimal fractions &c. There are many (other) questions to be answered but I must defer (them) till another opportunity.

I am, Dear Sir,

Your most assured friend

and obedient servant,

FRAM. WILLIS.

Caius College,
 Aug: 17, 1767."

4.

"Dear Sir.

One of the questions proposed for me to answer, in your letter of the 3rd of this month was, what studies I have been principally engaged in since my admission. In order to answer this I must tell you that we have a number of exhibitions here from £3 to £10 per annum each, which are divided among the freshmen every year, according to their several abilities. The candidates chuse some particular book, in which for three days they are to be

closely examined by the master and fellows,
or at least by such of them as like the office.
During this time of probation it is customary
with us, and has been so ever since the days
of Dr Caius, to have sugar-roll and sack standing
in the hall, and battledores and shuttlecocks
to divert ourselves with, while we are not
engaged with the fellows ; Joyous doings !

Ἡμεῖς δὲ κλέος οἶον ἀκουομεν, οὐδέ τι ἴδμεν.

There is a specimen of the old bard who
has taken up all my time ever since my
admission.   I hope to make myself entirely
master of him before I go into Suffolk.   You
ought to know whether such a custom prevails
in Magdalen, and if it does, you should take
care to make yourself acquainted very intimately
with one of the Classics whichever you please.
I have been somewhat more gay and idle than I
should have been this last fortnight, in making
parties to go on the water, and in riding out
to Newmarket and the country round about
Cambridge in little one-horse chaises, which
they call Bougeès (? Buggy).   This is a very
pleasant way of making a journey ; and going
upon the water with a set of no more than
four friends for about three miles to drink tea
is what I like exceedingly ; but have been
once caught in a violent shower of rain and
ducked pretty frequently.   If you are fond of
going on the water you will have a fine
opportunity of indulging your inclination, as
Magdalen is close by the river side, and the
men of Magdalen from being so much on
the water are called Magdalen rats.

A List of the fashionable terms in Cambridge with their meanings:

To shark or shirk - to break an appointment.
To go out - - - - to blush or look confounded.
To fag hard -   - to plod ; to study closely.
To drench - - - to pour liquor down a person's throat.
To job - - - - - to reprimand.
To send a man to Coventry - to refuse speaking to a man.
A jobation - - - a reprimand from a superior to an inferior.

I shall have a horse to ride out on with a servant of the Doctor's when I go to Weston, and if Banham be not too far off I shall certainly do myself the pleasure of calling upon you. I have been just now looking in the map and it seems to be but a very little way from Weston. I am extremely rejoiced to hear that your uncle visits Dr. Thurston, and hope by means of that acquaintance we may be often together. I shall go on next Wednesday.

I am, Dear Sir,
Yours sincerely,
FRAM WILLIS.

Caius College,
    Aug. 29, 1767."

5.

" Dear Sir,
    On Tuesday I received a letter from you, but without any date ; however as you seem

desirous that it should be answered without delay, I take the opportunity of to-day's post to write to you. It sometimes happens that sheets go with the bed, but more frequently they do not; for most people bring up new sheets with them at their first coming to College, and you may easily conceive that after they have been used 3 or 4 years they are worth but little to the next inhabitant of the room. If you bring up any with you, they should be two pair of small sheets. The rest of the linen you will want are two table-cloths, two breakfast cloths, some napkins and 6 towels and as many coarse cloths by way of rubbers. As to bands I do not think you can have them made to your liking in the country.

I have seen the Mr Tyson you speak of, at Dr Barnadiston's. He has very much of the gentleman in him, and is so good a classic that he sat for the medal. I saw a picture of him at the same time; a very good one in my opinion.

I had the pleasure of seeing Mr Buxton's house while I was in that part of the world; but as I went to dine with him and not with a professed intention of seeing the house, I did not perhaps see so many of the good pictures as you did. Mr. Buxton seemed to be a man who has some regard to the antiquity of his family. All the paintings I saw were in two parlours and most of them family ones.

In your next I hope to hear on what day we are to expect you here. The proctors for this year have declared their intention of being very assiduous in keeping up the University discipline.

I am, Dear Sir,
Your most obedient servant and friend,
FRAM. WILLIS.

Caius College,
October 13th, 1767."

COLLEGE LIFE AND WAYS SIXTY YEARS AGO.

[The substance of the following paper was read to the members of a College Club a few years ago. It may serve as a sort of Appendix to the foregoing historical essays, by showing how, and when, some of the various steps were taken by which the old order gradually died out. It must be remembered that for me, and my contemporaries, the medieval, or rather the Elizabethan, statutes were in full legal force. The University statutes had been but little changed; those of the Colleges not at all. So far as the law was concerned, we lived under the old régime. The remarks which follow were intended to show how far custom, as distinguished from law, had advanced from the old state of things towards that now familiar to every student. It need not be said that they are the reminiscences of a "reading man." (The late Mr. Henry Labouchere, of "Truth," almost over-lapped me in point of time; but I take it that his reminiscences would not have overlapped mine.)]

I have been asked to give some account of the manners and customs, the ways of thought, and the main teaching influences, prevalent in College in my day.

One natural preconception I should like to remove out of the way at once. I am not proposing to point a moral by drawing comparisons; that is to say, I do not want to pose as an advocate of either the ancient or the modern. Each advocate can find plenty to say for himself by appeal to familiar quotations. The old man may draw out a saying from his school-books which begins with "Ætas

parentum . . ."; the young man may retort
with a remark which is older still, and remind
us that he who asserts that the former days were
better than these "doth not enquire wisely."
We might go on all night pelting each other
with similar saws and rival authorities.

Sixty years represents a long stretch in
modern times. It embraces the period not
quite of your grandfathers, but one which extends some way behind that of most of your
fathers. It may almost seem to you as if the
inferences belonged to what are called the
"prehistoric" class; were of the kind which
depend upon the polish of chipped flints, and
the size and proportions of the crania of such
specimens as have happened to be preserved to
your own days. Doubtless I am a fossil; but
then I need not remind those of you who are
students of natural science how much may be
learnt from a fossil. Think what it would be if
some Pterodactyle or Ichthyosaurus—to go no
further back than that—could be induced to
give you a verbal account of its actual habits
and its former environment!

To begin, then, I apprehend that actual
College life played a larger part in our experience than it does in yours. For one thing
we were in residence for a considerably longer
time. Every man, "Poll" and "Honour" alike,
stayed here for ten terms before he was entitled
to a degree; that is, he had just half a year
more of residence. Again, almost every reading
man spent his Long Vacation here; moreover
he had three of these, instead of two, and the

Vacation residence embraced on the average nine weeks as against the present six. This statement does not rest on mere recollection. I went carefully into the question some years ago by reference to our cooks' books, which record the exact residence of every man, and I found that on the average the men of my time spent some twelve weeks more in Cambridge than do those of the present day: reckoning to the usual time of degree. This represents a large percentage in three years. And even as regards the Long Vacation, we were already on the down grade. Our nine weeks were what was left of an original allowance of twelve. This reduction had, I apprehend, been made just before my time, Dr. Phear, of Emmanuel, assures me that, in his first summer of coaching (1851) the four pupils who were reading with him stayed continuously for twelve weeks.

Then, too, we were hardly ever away for a single night. Except for the emergency of a call home, on account of illness or other grave cause, it never occurred to us to be absent from Cambridge during the course of actual term. In those days, as you perhaps know, the apparition of a telegram generally indicated death or some serious domestic crisis. The two main railways were of course then in existence—though the Great Northern route to Cambridge was hardly discovered — but the trains were comparatively few, slow, and expensive. A Great Eastern Sunday train took three-and-a-half hours from London to Cambridge—I suppose that many of you could beat this now by the road; on bicycles, of course, without appeal to the motor. Our early dinner-hour also stood in the way of any attempt to secure even a half-day away from Cambridge. From the nature of the case travelling was somewhat of a luxury. "Third Class" was out of the question, as that involved the "Parliamentary train," which stopped at every station. Even the second class carriages were most uncomfortable. The first class fare was twelve shillings; the same that it had been for an outside place on the coach.

As to education or tuition. The floodgates which might be supposed intended to pen in the exuberant energy of the lecturer had not then been opened, and no inundation of that kind yet threatened to cover the face of the earth. Of course we had College lectures, but then we had none but these. The inter-collegiate system was as yet unknown; in fact I am in the habit of priding myself on the claim of having been the first to introduce it into the University, some fifty years ago, in my own department of the Moral Sciences. Everyone, so far as the regular official instruction was concerned, was thus entirely dependent upon his own College. The obvious consequences followed. His own College may have provided well, say, in Mathematics, but have been utterly insufficient in every other direction. Outside Trinity and St. John's there was probably not a single College which provided what would now be considered the minimum of necessary instruction, even in Classics and Mathematics. Our own College was, I imagine, rather above the average in this respect, for the teachers were competent so far as the two main branches were concerned; but outside this narrow range all was a blank. Theology, for instance, was represented by a good-natured mathematician—his good nature being the cause of his accepting a post declined by his colleagues. He did not dive so deep into his subject as to consult Alford's Greek Testament, the ordinary popular hand-book of the day; and his grotesque attempts at[1] comment and interpretation, when he trusted to his own critical instincts, were the joke of the College. I shall not easily forget the feeling of being distinctly set back towards school-boyhood, experienced by those even who, like myself, had come from a second-rate school, but who had at any rate some familiarity with the Greek Testament. To a man like the late Professor Bensly, who came here straight from the admirable teaching at King's College, London, the experience must have been like that of waking up to find himself sitting on the benches of a Sunday school.

I have said that the teachers, classical

---

[1] It is one of the ironies of things that, whilst many learned and ingenious comments, from other teachers, have dropped out of mind, such an illustration as the following is retained. The lecturer was expounding the miracle of the healing of the paralytic recorded by St. Mark. He pointed out that as the subject was called a young man (τεκνον) he could not have been quite grown up: on the other hand, as it took four to carry him, he could not have been very young: " whence we may conclude that he was something between the two."

S

and mathematical, were competent. But they worked on a system which will rather surprise you. The "Little-Go" then occurred just in the middle of our career, and we had in consequence regular and frequent lectures both in classics and mathematics. During the first few terms we had to attend these every day from 9 to 11. So far, good; but what will now seem odd is that we all alike had to attend the same lecture. There was no selection or discrimination whatever. I imagine that the initial difference in the relative attainments of the freshmen was decidedly greater in those days than it is now, for there was no attempt at anything which could be called an entrance examination. So for term after term we all sat side by side, listening—or not listening, as the case may be— to the same exposition. There was, as I say, no selection or discrimination. The brilliant scholar from the best public schools, and the young man who had given up business and was beginning his Greek letters with a view to taking Orders; the destined high wrangler, who had read his conic sections as a schoolboy, and the youth to whom Euclid and his mysterious pictures were a daily puzzle, sat side by side on the benches of our lecture room, and tried to make the most of the lecture, or at any rate of the time during which the lecture was delivered. This arrangement, prevalent I believe in most if not in all the Colleges, was probably one of the worst features in the system of the day. It compelled every student, practically, to resort to a private tutor, for the lecturers, as a general rule, gave no assistance whatever out of their official hours. In fact, as they were very frequently private tutors as well, in their spare time, it could hardly be expected that they should do so. I feel quite confident that I never received a single word of advice during my whole time from the tutor, unless it were as to what church I had better attend or avoid. Under the circumstances of our lecture system you will understand that it was quite natural to say, as one came out of the room, "Now I can begin my work"; and that no sarcasm was intended when we agreed that one great advantage of the Long Vacation was that we were then entirely unhindered by lectures.

This absence of specialisation continued for a year, at least, after entry at College : I might almost say, for a year and a half. The Little-Go came, for all alike, at the end of the fifth term, and therefore our classics had to be kept up to some extent during fully half our career. More than this. During our first two terms those who hoped for a scholarship found it necessary to divide their attention almost equally between the two main subjects. It may be one of the perversities to which the old are notoriously subject, but I must confess to a preference of the former system over the latter, at any rate in this particular respect. Unless a man is being trained to become (say) a mathematical professor, I do not see any intellectual advantage in his "getting rid of" his classics at the outset. And I should say the same about most of the other professional or semi-professional subjects included in our various Triposes.

The Classical and Theological Examination came at the end of the first Lent term, the Mathematical at the end of the first May term. We were all classed for each of these, and the scholarships were awarded entirely by the joint results of the two examinations. With the exception of two or three petty encouragements to chemistry and anatomy there was no such thing in the College as a scholarship for any special subject. This was not a peculiarity in our case; it was almost universal in Cambridge. The old conception still prevailed that the scholarship was given in accordance with general attainments in the common subjects of the University course.

I alluded just now to the non-existence of what are called " open " scholarships. Considering how readily the clever boy obtains a scholarship nowadays at the age of 14 at any of our big schools, it will seem rather surprising to you that we at Cambridge had to wait till the end of our first year before we had a chance of such a distinction. And it will be the more surprising when we remember that at some Colleges at Oxford the modern system of open scholarships was already in vogue. The results of this difference of practice deserve notice. Take my own case. Two or three of my comrades obtained scholarships at Oxford Colleges, and for months before they left school enjoyed the consequent distinction, and their master the consequent credit. I, who was destined for

Cambridge, could not look forward to any such promotion till a year and a half later. I need hardly point out that, in these days of publicity and rivalry amongst the schools and their masters, such a disparity of conditions would have produced an almost insurmountable handicap in favour of Oxford. As it was, a strong inducement was offered to every clever boy to have a try there first. A few years after my time the consequences became so obvious that Cambridge was driven, in self-defence, to adopt the same system. If I may use terms which are risky in times of controversy, I should say that the preferential tariff on the Isis led to retaliation on the Cam, and that this retaliation was justified by its success.

The fact is, that the modern conception of a scholarship (or fellowship, for that matter) as a pure reward for intellectual merit or industry, and as a test therefore, to be widely advertised, of the schoolmaster's labour and skill, though already generally adopted in practice, had not yet been fully worked out into its consequences. I am not going either to attack or to defend that conception, but simply to point out that the ancient view, viz. that such endowments are purely charitable gifts — assistance intended solely for the poor student—was not altogether extinct. A free gift of course is judged by rules very different from those which are applied to prizes after competition. The donor, in the former case, gives to those who are in some way connected with him, to men of "founder's kin," to students from his own county, town, or school; and no rational person can object to his doing so. In my day, for instance, there were many scholarships, all of more or less ancient foundation, and nearly all confined to this or that locality. I happened to be the first scholar of my year, but the best scholarship was not then available for me. It had to go to someone from Norfolk. Of course there were complaints against such a state of things, and a few years later the growing revolt against these and other anomalies led to the first University Commission, which carried out such sweeping changes. It was this Commission, as you perhaps know, which first avowedly and statutably fixed the principle that University benefactions were to be regarded as rewards of intellectual merit, and of that only. As I have said, there was decided dissatisfaction felt by those who suffered under the old system; but I should hardly say that this amounted, as it would now, to a keen sense of definite injustice. One took these things, as one does most of the long-established mischiefs of the world, as something which would be better mended, but which did not call for loud complaint and outcry.

The elder Mr. Weller, you may remember, rather prided himself on the educational advantages which he had conferred upon his better-known son; he had, he said, just let him run about the streets and pick up information for himself. The College authorities of my day adopted a somewhat similar plan. In all respects we were left very much to ourselves in the matter of our studies. The tutor, Mr.

Clayton, never lectured. We saw him for a few minutes at the beginning and end of term; that is, to report our arrival and to secure our exeats. That comprised our whole intercourse with him, except perhaps an invitation, once or twice in the year, to a big breakfast party, or to the tea which led up to some missionary or religious meeting. To prevent any wrong impression I should like to say that this was not due to indolence or neglect. He was a very kind-hearted and worthy man; and I am convinced that if any of us had gone to him in difficulty or in doubt, he would have given all the assistance in his power. But that was not the custom. Moreover he had the charge of a populous parish in the town; and as the leading representative of the Evangelical party, he was much occupied in religious movements. I feel as certain as one can be that during my first two years I never had a word of private conversation with any authority of the College as to my studies, and equally sure that I never paid an informal visit to any Fellow's rooms. We selected our coaches by mutual advice and comparison; we decided for ourselves what line of studies we would follow. In saying this, however, it is only fair to remind you that our path was a much simpler one than yours. We had small alternative as to the choice of subjects, or as to the time of examination. There were only two goals for the Honour man, the Classical and the Mathematical. On this point I should like to add a few words. Every one knows that the advance of Natural Science, in respect of the number of teachers, and of the amount of lecture room, laboratory, and apparatus required, has been very great during the last 60 years. But I doubt whether you all recognize *how* great it has been. Put it in this way. As you walk down Pembroke Street you see some seven or eight acres to right and left of you, covered with buildings devoted to " Science." That is the grown, or rather the growing, tree : What was the seedling 60 years ago from which it has developed? I should say that it was a small table, such as two people might take their tea at; a table not in constant use, but brought into the Arts School three times a week during the May term. This will need some explanation. I am not speaking of the medical schools; and exception must be made of the Sedgwick Geological Museum, which already existed on the ground floor of the Cockerell Building in the University Library. But it is more than epigrammatically true of all the other modern departments. The performer at that table was Professor Stokes during his lectures on Physical Optics. He had the use of the room just for the purpose of his lectures. In 1856, when I attended, an assistant followed him with a heliostat, a prism, and one or two similar articles, which were placed on the table, and removed at the end of the lecture. Very likely he had more apparatus in his college rooms, but that was all that we students knew of. It is possible that Miller, the professor of Mineralogy, and

Henslow, of Botany, adopted similar devices; but I have some doubts as to this. Willis, the Jacksonian professor, had, I am told, a collection of mechanical models; but there was no museum in which to keep them. Whatever, and wherever, they may have been, however, they may be regarded similarly as the seedling from which the goodly tree of the present Engineering Department, with its Laboratory and range of workshops, has grown.

It is a moot point—which I am not going to discuss—whether, in our early years, the effort of study, or the actual result obtained, deserves most consideration. If the former, we had perhaps some advantages. How the Poll-men fared I can't say; by the results of the class-lists, I should judge, badly. As to Honour-men: we had few or no "tips" or notes of lectures, or suggestions as to what books or parts of books we should read. There was but little of this, I think, from the private tutors, and nothing, I should say, from the lecturer. The familiar Paley, of the Little-Go, may serve as an illustration. As we drifted on to the time when he became imminent we—I am speaking for my friends as well as for myself—procured the book and read it for ourselves. I never had a word of lecture upon him, and never saw a "tip" or sheet, beyond a few hints in the way of *memoria technica*, which tradition has doubtless handed on. Perhaps it was due to this mode of treatment that I found the book decidedly interesting, and still retain more than a lingering liking for Paley.

Those who are enquiring into the habits and beliefs of some almost extinct race of early culture naturally ask in the first place about their marriage customs, or the position of women amongst them, and about their religious rites. In our community the question is easily answered, for there were practically no ladies in the place, so far as we undergraduates were concerned. My cousin, Leslie Stephen, of Trinity Hall, who was three years my senior, used to say that about the only lady he had ever spoken to during his College course was, he believed, his bedmaker. I have tried to recall the occasions on which I was introduced to ladies' society—as I have said, for matters of this sort my memory is good—and can only remember three or four, and these were not exactly lively functions. The female element in University society was epigrammatically described as consisting of five or six wives of Masters of Colleges,[1] who sat apart; of five or

[1] The ancient dignity and inaccessibility of the Master of a College still lingered about the members of that order. Whewell was perhaps the last to retain the old attitude, which he did till his death in 1866. Towards the end of his life I had the following experience. A first cousin of mine was staying at the Lodge, and I received an invitation from her to come in and take a cup of tea on the Sunday evening. On arrival, the man-servant pointedly suggested that I should keep my gown on. As I was then an M.A. of five or six years' standing, I rather resented this requirement, and went into the drawing room as I was, in ordinary black. There was no party: only two cousins of mine, and Whewell himself—who did not wear a gown. The Master said nothing, whatever he looked; but next day I received a serious remonstrance from my cousin, evidently inspired by the Master, pointing out, courteously but severely, the gravity of the offence. Some years before this, when a small boy, I was taken by my father on a visit to the Lodge at Queens':—the

six wives of professors, upon whom the former
did not call; and of one other lady, wife of a
well-known classical coach. Remember, too,
that there was no May Week (or fortnight) in
those times.[2] The flower show, which was
started, I think, in my second year, was the sole
representative of that chronic festive activity
which becomes acute during the first half of
June. No one went to see the boat races otherwise than on foot; society, indeed, had not
clearly ascertained that Cambridge had a river.
I suppose that most men received a visit, once
during their career, from their parents and
sisters. But I should not like to be positive
on this, and I cannot recall more than a single
occasion on which I met the family of any friend
of mine. My own people came to see me once,
for a couple of days, in the Long Vacation.

As to orthodoxy, it is difficult, in these days
of free discussion, to bring home to you how
undisturbed we—that is, the average quiet
reading men—were in this direction. Atheism
of course had a certain vogue in the big cities,
but in those days it went in its shirt-sleeves
and corduroys, and smoked coarse tobacco; it

President was a contemporary and old friend of his. I
noticed that his sons, boys of somewhat my age, made a bow
on entering the room where their father was. This may
have been partly parental reverence, but I suspect it was
mainly magisterial authority which was recognized.

[2] Time was when Sturbridge Fair must have afforded, for
several weeks in September, as gay a time as any student or
visitor could have desired. But long before my time it had
sunk from being one of the great historic fairs of Europe,
recognized by, and feasted at, by University authorities, into
a two or three days' gathering of horse-dealers, circus per-
formers, and so forth.

had not come to cigars and dress-suits, and to sitting at table with bishops. I should say that the first tremor which foretold the coming earthquake was the publication of *Essays and Reviews* a year or two after I had graduated. What emphasized the influence of this rather dull production was the startling review of it by Mr. Frederic Harrison in the *Westminster*. As a rule, no sceptical remarks met our eyes in print. Amongst papers of repute there was indeed the *Leader*, a weekly newspaper, and the *Westminster Quarterly* just referred to, but they had no circulation here, and lay quite outside the path of most of us. Indeed, I think the existence of "the infidel" was only made known to us by his occasional demolition in orthodox polemical works. This was my own case, the orthodox writer being Rogers, the once well-known and popular author of the *Eclipse of Faith*. A decided majority of us—in our College at least—contemplated taking Orders, or had come to College with that hope on the part of their parents. Nearly half of us were sons of clergymen.

We were a very church-going, sermon-attending folk. Hall, on Sundays, was at 4. Chapel at 6. Accordingly, we came out of our own service during the course of that in the churches; and a very large number of us were in the habit of attending the sermon at one or other of the parish churches. Trinity Church was the most popular. It was then held by our tutor, Clayton, the representative of evangelical opinions here, who drew large

numbers of University men. He held the living
once occupied by Simeon, and carried on the
traditions thence established. The intermediate
link between the two was Carus. Harvey
Goodwin, afterwards Bishop of Carlisle, was
his only rival in popularity. But almost every
church in the town had its regular or
occasional visitors.

As to one prominent characteristic difference
between the old and the new, I feel a difficulty
in the want of a descriptive word that shall be
perfectly neutral. If we speak of your life as
being "luxurious," blame seems implied of the
present; and if we speak of our life as "simple"
or "severe," praise seems implied of the past.
Perhaps, therefore, it is best to speak generally
of the "ease" of modern life in College. Of
course this characteristic is not confined to
College life; it is displayed everywhere in every
detail of present society; it is the natural
and necessary outcome of improved mechanical
methods and advanced scientific knowledge.
Vastly more result is obtained by the average
labour of the average man, and this gain is
taken out in increased ease and comfort nearly
all round.

There is no question, then, that our life, in
comparison with yours, was somewhat rude and
severe. Begin with the meals. The Hall, in
my first year, was for freshmen at 4, for others
at 5; on Sundays, I think, for all alike, at 4.
Consideration of the restraints imposed upon
the digestive apparatus even of the young will
suggest that such an hour precluded, as a rule,

any serious attempt at either lunch or supper; and of course it blotted out all thought of 5 o'clock tea. It was not intended for this purpose, but was the temporary outcome of the well-known secular drift onwards of the dinner hour. Under Edward VI. that hour had been about 11; now it is 7 or 8; with us it was 4 or 5. Personally I hold that 5 p.m. was a very suitable hour for purposes of study; but it was decidedly hostile to the natural designs of the butcher. Lapsing for a moment into auto-biography, I should say that breakfast did not often go much beyond eggs and bacon; that lunch (if the term may be used) was secured by cutting bread and cheese at the cupboard door; and that the place of supper was occupied by tea and bread and jam. And the dinner itself was of the simplest. Nothing was regularly provided for the table beyond joints, potatoes and cabbage. There were, of course, waiters in hall,—gyps and bed-makers—but we did all our carving for ourselves, pushing the dish from one to another in turn. The wasteful hacking of the joints which ensued, may be conceived; as each operator followed out his own ideas as to the method of carving. (There is an engraving representing a dinner in Trinity, date about 1830, which will illustrate some of these details. During the 25 years or so which had elapsed, by my time, the custom of dressing for dinner had dropped out.) Sweets and cheese had to be specially ordered — "sized for," in technical vocabulary. Soup, fish and game were absolutely unknown. Let me add, though, that, to the best of my belief, such a being as a "teetotaller"[1] was not to be seen or heard of in the whole College.

As regards our rooms, of course furniture was scanty and plain for the most part; but the main difference was displayed in the bed-rooms. These were historically interesting as "survivals" of ancient conditions of life. As some of you know—I have gone into the subject in my *College History*—the very notion of a separate bedroom was a comparatively late introduction into College life. I should doubt if a single bedroom had a fire-place, except where an original entire chamber had been converted into a bedroom. Sometimes the sleeping apartment had been obtained by making a sort of hutch in the corner of the sitting room, separated off by a lath and plaster partition; sometimes a whole neighbouring chamber had been annexed for the purpose; sometimes one of the ancient "studies" in the corner of the main room was retained. There was one bedroom in which, literally, a man of six feet could not stand up; another, in which he could hardly lie down; in several, a bath

---

[1] A few years after this, when dining at Trinity, my host pointed out two Fellows at one of the tables, with the remark "They are teetotallers": somewhat in the tone in which he would have indicated, say, Parsees. There was a pernicious practice in college of giving beer-orders. One wrote a sort of cheque payable (in beer) to bearer. Armed with this the college servant, or other recipient of a tip, went to the buttery and was duly regaled. As some of them (e.g. the boot-black) came, to every man every term, for this purpose, the results were undesirable. I once asked that functionary how ever he managed to get through it. He could only reply, "We works it off, Sir, we works it off."

was impossible unless you balanced it on the bed. In my case, in the ancient Perse Buildings, a top attic—once doubtless shared between two students—had been set apart for a bedroom; so that I went up two pair of stairs to bed. It was under the thin sloping roof, with one window to the north. In the terribly severe winter of 1854-5 the water in the jug was frozen apparently into a solid block for several weeks, and my sponge became as a brickbat. Such washing as could be effected was carried on over the sitting-room fire. Apropos of this, I remember a man remarking, during this or a following winter, that he had thrown his sponge through the wall of his room. Regard had to the flimsy nature of some of the partition walls, as described above, and to the consistency which a sponge could sometimes acquire in college bedrooms, the statement was probably quite true.

I have said something about this elsewhere, but as it may be new to some of you I may devote a few words to giving a notion of our sanitary standard. In the bedroom above described I contracted small-pox. Of course the doctor (it was Paget—afterwards well-known as Sir George Paget, who was naturally aware what College rooms were like) at once ordered my bed to be brought down into the sitting-room; but what I want to point out is the sort of precautions against the spread of infection, which it was thought necessary to adopt. My sitting-room was one of six on the staircase. Not a man left in consequence;

disinfectants and antiseptics were quite unknown; no nurse was brought in; the bedmaker,
in her daily rounds, looked after my wants in
the intervals between attending on those of my
neighbours; and the tutor dropped in once or
twice to see how I was getting on. I just desired
a paper, with "Ware Small Pox" on it, to be
stuck on my door, and that was all. Of course it
was not a very severe case, but I know I felt
bad enough, and was in bed for a week or two.
I may add that mine was one of three or four
simultaneous cases, all similarly and success-
fully treated by the above simple method. Nor
did I ever hear that the bed-makers, or their
"helps," spread the mischief amongst their
own families in Barnwell or elsewhere. There
was nothing to call an epidemic in the place
in consequence of this. The infection had
been introduced by a medical student from
the hospital, where there were then several
cases.

No water was laid on anywhere in the
College. Our whole supply, for drinking and
washing, came from two or three pumps. One
of these stood at the corner of the Perse
Building, against the wall of the Fellows'
garden, and we used to hear the bedmakers
pumping and gossiping under our windows
during the greater part of the morning hours.
It may be added that almost exactly behind
this pump, on the other side of the wall, was
a privy in full use. Some years afterwards,
when the constant service had been introduced
from the waterworks, we had our first invasion

T

of a typhoid epidemic: due, as it happened, entirely to the introduction of poison germs in the drinking water.

What was done then, you may ask, in case of fire? As it happens, I can tell you, as the last serious fire in our College occurred during my second or third year. Our methods here, though—like those for the treatment of small-pox—somewhat out of date, were not quite ineffective. One evening, about nine o'clock, the bedmaker rushed into my room to say that the College Hall was on fire. I was one of the first to arrive. The floor was alight underneath, and the flames were streaming up against the wall from behind the wainscot. Incidents of the kind were sufficiently frequent and recent—there had been a big fire at Trinity Hall two or three years before—for tradition to prompt us aright. We ran back for our slop pails, and formed a line; several being told off to work the pumps. My station was near the top of the stairs, from which I could see the fire, apparently gaining ground. However, the supply of water soon became ample, and we extinguished the fire in time, partly owing to the exertions of an athletic fellow of the College, "Joe" Croker, who broke open the floor with a pickaxe so as to let the water reach the flames. For colleges on the river bank matters were much easier, as water in abundance could easily be obtained. Archdeacon Hare, in his sketch of John Sterling's Life, describes how, during a fire in the New Court of Trinity, he found his pupil—at that time in delicate health—heading

the line of buckets or pails by standing nearly
up to his middle in the water.

I add a few trifling matters because, after all,
the amenities of life are largely made up of a
multitude of petty details. Cabs, for instance,
to convey one to the playfields, or to an evening
entertainment, were quite unknown. They did
not begin to ply in the streets till many years
afterwards, and of course no one ever dreamt of
ordering out a fly from the hotel. I am tolerably
sure that I was scarcely once inside any conveyance except the omnibus, which at the beginning
and end of term took one from and to the station.

In those days of the paper-tax "the Press"
for us was represented by the books we bought,
or took out from the Union, or the newspapers
that we read there or at the booksellers'. You
might have searched the whole College through,
I suppose, without finding a periodical or journal
of any sort, except in the Fellows' Combination
Room or Master's Lodge. Cheap magazines—I
mean those at 1s., not at 3d.—started with
Macmillan in 1859. What we read, therefore,
were books. Doubtless, if the *Strand* or *Windsor*
had been procurable I should have read it; as it
was, I remember, I took to Alison's *History of
Europe* and similar works, and spent my spare
time in the two terms preceding the Little-Go
in learning German. A moderate supply of
novels could be procured from the Union
library; for the stern rule of excluding fiction,
with which the Society started, had been
abrogated before my time.

Our etiquette as to dress was rather strict.

The "chimney-pot" hat was our only head-gear besides the College cap, at first; but during my time it began to give way to what would now be called a "bowler" of some sort. The straw hat was a licence tolerated during the Long Vacation: I remember a man pointing to a comrade, who had dared to appear in a straw, at the beginning of the October term, and remarking that "he ought not to do that." Readers of *Verdant Green* may remember that when the hero of that story went to Oxford— just about the time that I came to Cambridge— the coach in which they travelled was lined out-side with *hat-boxes*. We always carried our silk hats with us, either in a box or on our heads. On the way to the boats, even, no man wore a flannel cap, still less a blazer.[1] On Sundays— but here the proctors set the rule—no one ever walked except in cap and gown; and accordingly the villages for ten miles round were familiar with the academic dress.

As to our modes of getting about the country —our private locomotion—you, of the bicycle period, may like to know how we effected it. I am the more willing to explain this because I belong to the now fast dwindling generation which actually practised the art I am about to describe. If you will give me your careful

---

[1] To speak of a "blazer" in the modern sense, *i.e.* as a flannel jacket of any colour, is, strictly speaking, an ana-chronism. We spoke only of "a Johnian blazer"; the bright scarlet of the Lady Margaret club making the application quite appropriate. The extension of the term, as at present, occurred soon afterwards. Can the athletic supremacy of the club (St. John's was head of the river 1854-7) have had any-thing to do with the change of application?

attention for a few moments I think I can make
it plain. Conceive yourself, then, on a bicycle,
from which the entire framework and both
wheels have been removed. And suppose that
instead of employing the feet indirectly to work
pedals they are brought to bear directly upon
the surface of the earth. You will see at once
that locomotion in this way is quite feasible,
though of course tedious and slow in comparison with the present method. We called
it "walking," and managed by this device to
accomplish considerable distances. Indeed,
there was a somewhat prevalent persuasion in
my time that the proper thing to do was to
walk to London in the day. A considerable
number of my contemporaries—some of whom
are still alive—fulfilled this duty. Indeed I,
who appear before you now, have done the
same. Doubtless you know the roads about
here as well as we did, and for many miles
outside what was familiar to us: but do you
know the country in directions where your
wheels are apt to be a hindrance? Two very
characteristic specimens of our local scenery
became early familiar to me, and would still
stand out vividly in my memory even if I had
not visited them since. One of these is the river-
way to Ely, along the towing-path. Never can
I forget the aspect of that lonely waste of
the fen-lands, as I first saw them in winter,
with the church spires standing out across
the level, against the evening sky. Another
such picture is that strange and grand
monument of early times, the Fleam Dyke,

from its commencement in the fens near
Fulbourn Station to where it is lost in the
woods toward Wood Ditton. Wild life, in some
of its forms, was not then so scarce as it is
now. For instance, a pair of ravens bred in
Madingley Park. And I have seen herons and
the green wood-pecker in the meadows beyond
Grantchester.

Apropos of the river, one or two reminiscences may be excused. I was always fond
of the strange and lonely reaches of the Cam
towards Ely. One long vacation, in August, I
walked with a friend, by the towing path, to
Ely. One curious fact struck us. There were
no gates on the path, but only solidly-built
stiles. The hoof-marks of the horses were plain
enough to within a few feet of the stile, and
recommenced in the same way a few feet
beyond. In the interval, what became of the
horses? Did they climb or did they jump?
It seemed incredible that such lumbering beasts
could be got over by such means. So we waited
at one stile to see. True enough, as the barge
advanced, the horses were stopped to allow the
rope to become slack. They were then whipped
up and made to jump. It was plain that they
sometimes failed to clear the stile, for the top
bar was scored with hoof-marks, and in some
cases had been solidly repaired. On enquiring
at a neighbouring farm-house we were told that
it was no use putting gates on the path, as
"those bargees" were such a rough lot that they
could never be trusted to shut them. (Shortly
afterwards I was struck by a remark in

Olmsted's work on the slave states of America.
Explaining the economical disadvantages of
slavery he pointed out that, owing to the
ignorance and coarseness of the negroes, they
could only be trusted with mules; horses would
soon be knocked up by their treatment.) Another habit of the bargees may be noticed, as
it may help to explain some old allusions and
pictures. In the times rather before mine the
barges were not usually, as now, punted through
the town and past the Colleges (see Ackerman's
picture of Clare College); the horses were
harnessed to the barge, and made to tow it,
the bargee sitting on the back of the horse. An
old uncle of mine who, as Fellow of Queens',
occupied rooms facing the river, retained to his
dying day recollections of the sufferings of the
horses and the lurid language of their drivers.
By my time the river had lost its old commercial importance as the sole means of access
for heavy goods, though it was probably more
used than it is now. Sedge, for instance, once
the sole material used for kindling, was still
brought up in barges from the Fens; and the
cry of "Sedge, Oh!" was to be heard of an
evening about the town. I suspect that the
present resined fire-lighters (like Huntley and
Palmer's Reading biscuits) were amongst the
"freshmen" who came up just before me, and
have been in residence ever since.

But there is more to be said on the subject
of walking. Remember that it was, with
the majority of us, the sole mode of exercise.
There was of course the river, for those who

had a taste that way, and there was some
cricket for a few weeks in May. But that
was all. Lawn tennis and croquet were unborn.
Real tennis and hunting were of course confined
to the wealthy few. Hockey and football were
left to boys. I have been since informed that
some devotees of what was commonly regarded
as a school game occasionally indulged, in
obscure places, in the peculiar art that they
had acquired at Rugby or Eton. But I am
certain that I never saw the game played,
and that no friend of mine ever practised
it. This is confirmed by my brother, who
was four years my junior. He tells me that
he remembers a friend coming in to Hall
and relating that he had seen a number of
Rugby men, mostly freshmen, playing a new
game: that "they made a circle round a ball
and butted each other." As to hockey, I
remember its being once referred to by a
Rugbeian: "Ah, a private school game." With
the exception then of those who boated, no
ordinary reading men ever did anything
in the afternoon but walk in the country.
Don't suppose that I am drawing invidious
comparisons, or underrating our disadvantages,
but I should like to point out one consequence
of such a state of things. I have been asked
before now what I had found to be the
main formative educational influences here. I
have replied, with strict truth, that I had
learnt something from my lecturers, more
from my coach, but most of all from conversation with friends; and the main opportunity

for such conversation was the daily walk.
What comes back to my mind most vividly
in such a connection? I am anticipating a
little in referring to John Seeley, for I did
not know him actually as an undergraduate,
though I became intimate with him soon
after. And what is the most vivid impression
of him that has been left stamped on my
mind? I should say, as the delightful
companion of a long day's walk. Memories
come crowding back to me of hours spent
on Welsh mountains, and in Yorkshire dales,
and over the breezy commons of Surrey, with
that most stimulating of companions by my
side: and all the time the incessant "give
and take" of conversation :—(it was nine
parts of "take" and one of "give," so far
as his comrades were generally concerned.)
Traditions of him may have come down to
you from those of middle standing who knew
him here. If so, the picture would be perhaps
of one with almost an excess of the philosophic
mind; grave, dignified, and possibly somewhat
lethargic. I wish I could adequately portray
the slim, active form of one who was then one
of the keenest and most subtle of dialecticians,
brimming over with happy illustration and
humourous fancy, and with a memory stored
with poetry and philosophy. Those were the
early fermenting years, when *Ecce Homo* was
taking shape in his mind. Ah, gentlemen!—
if I could set before you half-an-hour of his
conversation I should speak to more purpose
than I am likely to do now.

His, of course, is an extreme case, but many another walk is dotted with similar bright spots of reminiscence; and the level roads and lanes for miles round about us here in Cambridge serve to recall hours of delightful and profitable intercourse with many a dear friend of the past. I do not doubt that your interest in the problems of Ethics, Politics, and Philosophy is just as keen as ours, and that it exists with equal intensity during a scrimmage on the football field, or a lively rally at tennis, but it will be admitted that the free expression of that interest is comparatively hampered at the time.

INDEX.

INDEX.

Lightning Source UK Ltd.
Milton Keynes UK
UKOW04f1018020216

267590UK00001B/23/P